121
Ay24p

THE PROBLEM OF KNOWLEDGE

THE PROBLEM
OF
KNOWLEDGE

BY

A. J. AYER, M.A., F.B.A.

GROTE PROFESSOR OF THE PHILOSOPHY OF MIND
AND LOGIC IN THE UNIVERSITY OF LONDON

LONDON
MACMILLAN & CO LTD
NEW YORK · ST MARTIN'S PRESS
1956

MACMILLAN AND COMPANY LIMITED
London Bombay Calcutta Madras Melbourne

THE MACMILLAN COMPANY OF CANADA LIMITED
Toronto

ST MARTIN'S PRESS INC
New York

PRINTED IN GREAT BRITAIN

TO
MARY AND ROBIN CAMPBELL

PREFACE

IN this book I begin by taking the question of what is meant by knowledge as an example of a philosophical enquiry. Having maintained that to say that one knows a fact is to claim the right to be sure of it, I show how such claims may be disputed on philosophical grounds. Though their targets vary, these sceptical challenges follow a consistent pattern; the same line of reasoning is used to impugn our knowledge of the external world, or of the past, or of the experiences of others. The attempt to meet these objections supplies the main subject-matter for what is called the theory of knowledge; and different philosophical standpoints are characterized by the acceptance or denial of different stages in the sceptic's argument.

Having dealt in a general way with the question of scepticism and certainty, I pass to a detailed analysis of the philosophical problems of perception, memory, and one's knowledge of other minds. I do not suppose that I have said the last word upon any of these problems, but I hope that I have done something to clear the way for their solution. In the course of the book I also make some observations about philosophical method, the dimensions of time, causality, and personal identity. I have tried throughout to present my argument in a way that can be of interest to the general reader as well as to professional philosophers: but I have not tried to make my subject appear more simple than it is.

Some of the material which I have included in the

second and third chapters is also to be found in an article on 'Philosophical Scepticism' which I contributed to *Contemporary British Philosophy*, a collection of essays edited by Professor H. D. Lewis, and in an article on 'Perception' which I contributed to *British Philosophy in Mid-Century*, a collection edited by Professor C. A. Mace. I have to thank these editors and the publishers Messrs. Allen & Unwin for allowing me to reproduce the passages concerned. My thanks are due also to Mr. Richard Wollheim for his advice and criticism and to Miss Lindsay Darling for her help in making the index and correcting the proofs.

A. J. AYER

2 WHITEHORSE STREET
LONDON, W.1

December 1955

CONTENTS

CHAPTER I

PHILOSOPHY AND KNOWLEDGE

(i)

The method of philosophy

IT is by its methods rather than its subject-matter that philosophy is to be distinguished from other arts or sciences. Philosophers make statements which are intended to be true, and they commonly rely on argument both to support their own theories and to refute the theories of others; but the arguments which they use are of a peculiar character. The proof of a philosophical statement is not, or only very seldom, like the proof of a mathematical statement; it does not normally consist in formal demonstration. Neither is it like the proof of a statement in any of the descriptive sciences. Philosophical theories are not tested by observation. They are neutral with respect to particular matters of fact.

This is not to say that philosophers are not concerned with facts, but they are in the strange position that all the evidence which bears upon their problems is already available to them. It is not further scientific information that is needed to decide such philosophical questions as whether the material world is real, whether objects continue to exist at times when they are not perceived, whether other human beings are conscious in the same sense as one is oneself. These are not questions that can be settled by experiment, since the way in which they are answered itself determines how the result of any experiment is to be interpreted. What is in dispute in such cases is not whether, in a given set of circumstances, this or that event will happen, but rather how anything at all that happens is to be described.

This preoccupation with the way things are, or are to be, described is often represented as an enquiry into their essential nature. Thus philosophers are given to asking such questions as What is mind? What sort of a relation is causality? What is the nature of belief? What is truth? The difficulty is then to see how such questions are to be taken. It must not be supposed, for instance, that a philosopher who asks What is mind? is looking for the kind of information that a psychologist might give him. His problem is not that he is ignorant of the ways in which people think and feel, or even that he is unable to explain them. Neither should it be assumed that he is simply looking for a definition. It is not as if philosophers do not understand how words like 'mind' or 'causality' or 'truth' are actually used. But why, then, do they ask such questions? What is it that they are trying to find out?

The answer to this, though not indeed the whole answer, is that, already knowing the use of certain expressions, they are seeking to give an analysis of their meaning. This distinction between the use of an expression and the analysis of its meaning is not easy to grasp. Let us try to make it clear by taking an example. Consider the case of knowledge. A glance at the dictionary will show that the verb 'to know' is used in a variety of ways. We can speak of knowing, in the sense of being familiar with, a person or a place, of knowing something in the sense of having had experience of it, as when someone says that he has known hunger or fear, of knowing in the sense of being able to recognize or distinguish, as when we claim to know an honest man when we see one or to know butter from margarine. I may be said to know my Dickens, if I have read, remember, and can perhaps also quote his writings; to know a subject such as trigonometry, if I have mastered it; to know how to swim or drive a car; to know how to behave myself. Most important of all, perhaps, are the uses for which the dictionary gives the definition of 'to be aware or apprized of', 'to apprehend or comprehend as fact or truth', the sense, or senses, in which to have knowledge is to know that something or other is the case.

All this is a matter of lexicography. The facts are known, in a sense, to anyone who understands the English language, though not everyone who understands the English language would be competent to set them out. The lexicographer, *pace* Dr. Johnson, is required to be something more than a harmless drudge. What he is not required to be is a philosopher. To possess the information which the dictionary provides about the accredited uses of the English word 'to know', or the corresponding words in other languages, is no doubt a necessary qualification for giving an analysis of knowledge; but it is not sufficient. The philosopher who has this information may still ask What is knowledge? and hesitate for an answer.

We may discover the sense of the philosopher's question by seeing what further questions it incorporates, and what sorts of statement the attempt to answer it leads him to make. Thus, he may enquire whether the different cases in which we speak of knowing have any one thing in common; whether, for example, they are alike in implying the presence of some special state of mind. He may maintain that there is, on the subjective side, no difference in kind between knowing and believing, or, alternatively, that knowing is a special sort of mental act. If he thinks it correct to speak of acts of knowing, he may go on to enquire into the nature of their objects. Is any limitation to be set upon them? Or, putting it another way, is there anything thinkable that is beyond the reach of human knowledge? Does knowing make a difference to what is known? Is it necessary to distinguish between the sorts of things that can be known directly and those that can be known only indirectly? And, if so, what are the relationships between them? Perhaps it is philosophically misleading to talk of knowing objects at all. It may be possible to show that what appears to be an instance of knowing some object always comes down to knowing that something is the case. What is known, in this sense, must be true, whereas what is believed may very well be false. But it is also possible to believe what is in fact true without knowing it. Is knowledge then to be distinguished by the fact that if one knows that something is so, one cannot be mistaken? And in that case does it follow that what is known is necessarily true, or in some other way indubitable? But, if this does follow, it will lead in its turn to the conclusion that we commonly claim to know much more than we really do; perhaps even to the paradox that we do not know anything at all: for it may be contended that there is no statement whatsoever that is not in itself susceptible to doubt. Yet surely there must be something wrong with an argument that would make knowledge unattainable. Surely some of our claims to knowledge must be capable of being justified. But in what ways can we justify them? In what would the processes of justifying them consist?

I do not say that all these questions are clear, or even that they are all coherent. But they are instances of the sort of question that philosophers ask. The next step is to see how one would try to answer them. Once again, it will be best to take particular examples. Let us begin with the question whether the various sorts of knowing have any one thing in common, and the suggestion that this common feature is a mental state or act.

(ii)
Common features of knowledge

Except where a word is patently ambiguous, it is natural for us to assume that the different situations, or types of situation, to which it applies have a distinctive common feature. For otherwise why should we use the same word to refer to them? Sometimes we have another way of describing such a common feature; we can say, for example, that what irascible people have in common is that they are all prone to anger. But very often we have no way of saying what is common to the things to which the same word applies except by using the word itself. How else should we describe the distinctively common feature of red things except by saying that they are all red? In the same way, it might be said that what the things that we call 'games' have in common is just that they are games; but here there seems to be a difference. Whereas there is a simple and straightforward resemblance between the things whose colour we call 'red',

recognize objects without troubling to describe them, even to ourselves. No doubt, once we have acquired the use of language, we can always describe them if we choose, although the descriptions that we have at our command may not always be the descriptions that we want. 'I know that tune', I say, though its name escapes me and I cannot remember where I heard it before; 'I know that man', though I have forgotten who he is. But at least I identify him as a man, and as a man that I have met somewhere or other. There is a sense in which knowing something, in this usage of the term, is always a matter of knowing what it is ; and in this sense it can perhaps be represented as knowing a fact, as knowing that something is so.

Much the same applies to the cases where knowing is a matter of knowing how. Certainly, when people possess skills, even intellectual skills, like the ability to act or teach, they are not always consciously aware of the procedures which they follow. They use the appropriate means to attain their ends, but the fact that these means are appropriate may never be made explicit by them even to themselves. There are a great many things that people habitually do well, without remarking how they do them. In many cases they could not say how they did them if they tried. Nor does this mean that their performances are unintelligent. As Professor Ryle has pointed out,[1] the display of intelligence lies in the manner of the performance, rather than in its being accompanied or preceded by any conscious recognition of the relevant facts. The performer does not need to tell himself that if such and such things are done, then such and such will follow. He may, indeed, do so, but equally he may not : and

[1] G. Ryle, *The Concept of Mind*, ch. 2.

even when he does it is not because of this that his performance is judged to be intelligent. This point is convincingly established by Professor Ryle. But once again, if we are prepared to say that knowing facts need not consist in anything more than a disposition to behave in certain ways, we can construe knowing how to do things as being, in its fashion, a matter of knowing facts. Only by this time we shall have so extended our use of the expression 'knowing facts' or 'knowing that something is the case' that it may well become misleading. It may be taken to imply that the resemblances between the different ways of having, or manifesting, knowledge are closer and neater than they really are.

(iii)

Does knowing consist in being in a special state of mind?

It should by now be obvious that if 'knowing a fact' is understood in this extended sense, it need not be even partially a description of any special state of mind. But suppose that we confine our attention to the cases in which knowing something is straightforwardly a matter of knowing something to be true, the cases where it is natural in English to use the expression 'knowing that', or one of its grammatical variants. Is it a necessary condition for having this sort of knowledge, not only that what one is said to know should in fact be true, but also that one should be in some special state of mind, or that one should be performing some special mental act? Is it perhaps a sufficient condition, or even both necessary and sufficient? Some philosophers have maintained not only that there are such cognitive states, or acts, but that they are infallible. According to them, it is impossible for anyone to be in such a state of mind, unless what it purports to reveal to him is really so. For someone to think that he knows something when he really does not know it, it is not enough, in their view, that he should be mistaken about the fact which he claims to know, that what he thinks true should actually be false; he must also be mistaken about the character of his mental state: for if his mental state were what he took it to be, that is a state of knowledge, he could not be mistaken about the fact which it revealed to him. If this view were correct, then being in a mental state of this kind would be a sufficient condition for having knowledge. And if, in addition, one could not know anything to be true without being in this state, it would be both necessary and sufficient.

An obvious objection to this thesis is that to credit someone with the possession of knowledge is not to say that he is actually displaying it, even to himself. I know some facts of ancient history and I do not know them only on the rare occasions when I call them to mind. I know them at this moment even though I am not thinking of them. What is necessary is that if I were to think of them I should get them right, that if the subject comes up I am in a position to make statements which are authoritative and true. It is not necessary that I should continually be making these statements, or even that I should ever make them, provided that I could make them if the occasion arose. This point is sometimes made by saying that the verb 'to know' is used to signify a disposition or, as Ryle puts it, that it is a 'capacity' verb.[1] To have knowledge is to have the power to give a successful performance, not actually to be giving one.

[1] *Op. cit.* pp. 133-134.

But still, it may be said, however intermittent these performances may be, it is surely necessary that they be given at least once. They need not be public, but even if they are only private they must in fact occur. It would be absurd to say that someone knew a truth, which he had never even thought of, or one that he had thought of but not acknowledged to be true. Let it be granted that the most common use of the English verb 'to know' is dispositional. It is not even the only correct use — we do sometimes speak of knowing in the sense of coming to realize — but let that pass. The important point is that the dispositions which are taken to constitute knowing must sometimes be actualized. And the way in which they are actualized, so this argument continues, is through the existence of a special mental state.

But what is this state of mind supposed to be? The reply to this may be that it is unique in character, so that it cannot be analysed in terms of anything else. But what then is the evidence for its existence? It is indeed true that one is not reasonably said to know a fact unless one is completely sure of it. This is one of the distinctions between knowledge and belief. One may also be completely sure of what one believes, in cases where the belief is refused the title of knowledge on other grounds; such as that it is false, or that, although it is true, the reasons for which it is held do not come up to the standard which knowledge requires. But whereas it is possible to believe what one is not completely sure of, so that one can consistently admit that what one believes to be true may nevertheless be false, this does not apply to knowledge. It can, indeed, be said of someone who hesitates, or makes a mistake, that he really knows what he is showing himself to be unsure of, the implication being that he ought, or is in a position, to be sure. But to say of oneself that one knew that such and such a statement was true but that one was not altogether sure of it would be self-contradictory. On the other hand, while the respective states of mind of one who knows some statement to be true and another who only believes it may in this way be different, it does not seem that there need be any difference between them when the belief is held with full conviction, and is distinguished from knowledge on other grounds. As Professor Austin puts it, 'Saying "I know" is *not* saying "I have performed a specially striking feat of cognition, superior, in the same scale as believing and being sure, even to being merely quite sure": for there *is* nothing in that scale superior to being quite sure'.[1] And it may very well happen that even when people's beliefs are false they are as fully convinced of their truth as they are of the truth of what they know.

Moreover, though to be convinced of something is, in a sense, to be in a particular state of mind, it does not seem to consist in any special mental occurrence. It is rather a matter of accepting the fact in question and of not being at all disposed to doubt it than of contemplating it with a conscious feeling of conviction. Such feelings of conviction do indeed exist. There is the experience of suddenly coming to realize the truth of something that one had not known before: and it may be that similar experiences occur when one is engaged in defending a belief that has been put in question, or when one finally succeeds in resolving a doubt. But for the most part the things that we claim

[1] J. L. Austin, 'Other Minds', *Supplementary Proceedings of the Aristotelian Society*, vol. xx, p. 171.

to know are not presented to us in an aura of revelation. We learn that they are so, and from then on we unquestioningly accept them. But this is not a matter of having any special feelings. It is not certain that to have a feeling of conviction is even a sufficient condition for being sure ; for it would seem that a conscious feeling of complete conviction may co-exist with an unconscious feeling of doubt. But whether or not it ever is sufficient, it clearly is not necessary. One can be sure without it. And equally its presence is not necessary for the possession, or even for the display, of knowledge.

The fact is, as Professor Austin has pointed out,[1] that the expression 'I know' commonly has what he calls a 'performative' rather than a descriptive use. To say that I know that something is the case, though it does imply that I am sure of it, is not so much to report my state of mind as to vouch for the truth of whatever it may be. In saying that I know it I engage myself to answer for its truth : and I let it be understood that I am in a position to give this undertaking. If my credentials do not meet the usual standards, you have the right to reproach me. You have no right to reproach me if I merely say that I believe, though you may think the less of me if my belief appears to you irrational. If I tell you that I believe something which I do not, I am misinforming you only about my mental attitude ; but if I tell you that I know something which I do not, the chances are that I am misinforming you about the truth of the statement which I claim to know, or if not about its truth, then about my authority for making it. In the same way, to say of some other person that he knows that such and such is so is not

[1] *Op. cit.*

primarily, if at all, to describe his state of mind ; it is first of all to grant that what he is said to know is true ; and, secondly, it is to admit his credentials. If we consider that his credentials are insufficient, whether on the ground that he is not, as we say, in a position to know, though others might be, or, possibly, because we hold that what he claims to know is something for which neither he nor anyone could have the requisite authority, then we will not allow that he really does know what he says he knows, even though he is quite sure of it and even though it is actually true.

But here it may be objected that this excursus into philology is beside the point. Let it be granted that the expression 'I know' is not always used in English to signify a cognitive mental state. Let it be granted even, what is very much more doubtful, that it is never so used. The fact remains, it may be argued, that these cognitive states, or acts, exist. When they do occur, they are sufficient for knowledge. Furthermore, their existence is the only authority worth having, so that if our ordinary use of words were strictly philosophical, which it obviously is not, they would be not only sufficient for knowledge, but necessary as well.

Now I do not deny that ordinary usage is capable of improvement, or even that some improvement might be made in it on philosophical grounds. Philosophers, like scientists, are at liberty to introduce technical terms, or to use ordinary words in a technical sense. But this proposal to restrict the application of the verb 'to know' to cases where the knowledge consisted in someone's being in a cognitive mental state would not be fortunate. For the consequence of accepting it would be that no one could ever properly be said to know anything at all.

The reason for this is that there cannot be a mental state which, being as it were directed towards a fact, is such that it guarantees that the fact is so. And here I am not saying merely that such states never do occur, or even that it is causally impossible that they ever should occur, but rather that it is logically impossible. My point is that from the fact that someone is convinced that something is true, however firm his conviction may be, it never follows logically that it is true.[1] If he is a reliable witness and if he is in a good position to assess the truth of whatever statement is in question, then his being convinced of its truth may provide us with a strong reason for accepting it ; but it cannot be a conclusive reason. There will not be a formal contradiction in saying both that the man's state of mind is such that he is absolutely sure that a given statement is true, and that the statement is false. There would indeed be a contradiction in saying both that he knew the statement to be true, and that it was false ; but this, as has already been explained, is because it enters into the meaning of the word 'know' that one cannot know what is not true. It cannot validly be inferred from this linguistic fact that when someone is considering a statement which he knows to be true, it is his state of mind that guarantees its truth. The statement is true if, and only if, what it states is so, or, in other words, if the situation which it describes is as it describes it. And whether the situation really is as it is described is not to be decided merely by examining the attitude which anyone who considers the statement has towards it, not even if the person who considers it knows it to be true. If philosophers have denied, or

[1] Except in the rare cases when the truth of the statement in question is a logical condition of its being believed, as in the assertion of one's own existence. *Vide* Chapter II, section iii.

overlooked, this point, the fault may lie in their use of such expressions as 'state of knowledge'. For if to say of someone that he is in a state of knowledge is merely to describe his condition of mind, it does not entail that there is anything which he knows; and if it does entail that there is something which he knows, then, as we have seen, it does not merely describe his condition of mind. Since the expression is in any case artificial, it may be understood in either of these ways, though I suppose it would be more natural to take it in the second sense, as signifying the opposite of being in a state of ignorance. What we may not do is use it in both senses at once, for they are incompatible; an expression cannot refer only to a condition of mind, and to something else besides. The mistake should be obvious when it is pointed out, but it has not always been avoided. And the result is that a condition of mind, ambiguously referred to as a state of knowledge, is wrongly thought to be sufficient to guarantee the truth of the statements upon which it is supposed to be directed.

But unless some states of mind are cognitive, it may be said, how can we come to know anything? We may make the truth of some statements depend upon the truth of others, but this process cannot go on for ever. There must be some statements of empirical fact which are directly verified. And in what can this verification consist except in our having the appropriate experiences? But then these experiences will be cognitive: to have whatever experience it may be will itself be a way of knowing something to be true. And a similar argument applies to *a priori* statements, like those of logic or pure mathematics. We may prove one mathematical statement by deducing it from others, but the proof must start somewhere. There must be at least one statement which is accepted without such proof, an axiom of some sort which is known intuitively. Even if we are able to explain away our knowledge of such axioms, by showing that they are true by definition, we still have to see that a set of definitions is consistent. To conduct any formal proof, we have to be able to see that one statement follows logically from another. But what is this seeing that one statement follows from another except the performance of a cognitive act?

The bases of this argument are sound. We do just have to see that certain proofs are valid, and it is through having some experience that we discover the truth or falsehood of any statement of empirical fact. In the case of some such statements, it may even be that our having certain experiences verifies them conclusively. This is a point which will have to be considered later on. But in any such case what verifies the statement, whether conclusively or not, is the existence of the experience, not the confidence that we may have in some description of it. To take a simple example, what verifies the statement that I have a headache is my feeling a headache, not my having a feeling of confidence that the statement that I have a headache is true. Of course if I do have a headache and also understand the statement, I shall undoubtedly accept it as being true. This is the ground for saying that if I have such an experience, I know that I am having it. But, in this sense, my knowing that I am having the experience is just my having it and being able to identify it. I know that I am having it inasmuch as I correctly take it as verifying the statement which describes it. But my justification for accepting the statement is not that I have a cognitive, or any other attitude towards it : it is simply that I am having the experience. To say that the experience itself is cognitive is correct, though perhaps misleading, if it is merely a way of saying that it is a conscious experience. It may still be correct if it is a way of saying that the experience is recognized for what it is by the person who is having it, though, as we shall see later on, such recognition can be mistaken. It is not correct if it is taken as implying that the experience either consists in or includes a process of infallibly apprehending some statement to be true.

Similarly, what makes it true, for example, that the conclusion of a syllogism follows from the premises is that the inference exemplifies a law of logic. And if we are asked what makes the law of logic true, we can in this and in many other cases provide a proof. But this proof in its turn relies upon some law of logic. There will come a point, therefore, when we are reduced to saying of some logical statement simply that it is valid. Now to be in a position to say that such a statement is valid we must be able to see that it is so, but it is not made valid by our seeing that it is. It is valid in its own right. Of course if 'seeing' here has the force of 'knowing', then the fact that the statement is valid will indeed follow from the fact that it is seen to be so. But once again this makes only the verbal point, that we are not, in this usage, entitled to talk of 'seeing' something to be true unless it really is true. It does not prove that there are, or can be, any mental states of intuition which are such that their existence affords an absolute guarantee that one really is, in this sense, seeing what one thinks one sees. It must always remain possible that one is mistaken. Admittedly, if someone thinks that he may have been mistaken in accepting some logical statement which had seemed to him evidently true, there may be nothing for him to do but just look at it again. And if this second look confirms the first, his doubts may reasonably be put to rest. But the truth of the statement in question still does not logically follow from the fact that it continues to strike him as self-evident. Truths of logic make no reference to persons : consequently, they cannot be established by any mere description of some person's mental state. And this holds good whatever the mental state may be.

This is not to say that we do not know the truth of any *a priori* statements, or even that we do not know some of them intuitively, if to know them intuitively is to know them without proof. Our argument no more implies this than it implies that we cannot know any empirical statements to be true. It is designed to show, not that we do not have the knowledge which we think we have, but only that knowing should not be represented as a matter of being in some infallible state of consciousness : for there cannot be such states.

This point is important, if only because their neglect of it has led philosophers into difficulties which might have been avoided. In Berkeley's well-known phrase they 'have first raised a dust, and then complain, we cannot see'.[1] Starting from the premise that consciousness, in the sense of cognitive awareness, must always be consciousness *of* something, they have perplexed themselves with such questions as what consciousness is in itself and how it is related to the things,

[1] G. Berkeley, *The Principles of Human Knowledge*, Introduction, section iii.

or facts, which are its objects. It does not seem to be identical with its objects, yet neither does it seem to be anything apart from them. They are separate, yet nothing separates them. When there is added the further premise that consciousness is also self-conscious, the problem becomes more complicated still. In attempting to solve it existentialist philosophers have gone so far as to deny the law of identity and even to speak of 'the nothing' as if it were a special sort of agent, one of whose functions was to divide consciousness from itself. But apart from their own obvious demerits, these are reactions to a problem which should not arise. It depends upon the initial mistake of assuming that a naïve analysis in terms of act and object yields an adequate account of knowledge.

Other philosophers, besides the existentialists, have made the mistake of treating knowledge as though it consisted in the possession of an inner searchlight. How far, they then ask, can the searchlight reach? Is it confined to the present or can its rays illuminate the past? Is not remembering a way of knowing? But does it then follow that the past is still real? Perhaps the light can even play upon the future. But how can it be possible to inspect what does not yet exist? It is commonly assumed that we can train the searchlight upon our own conscious states. But can it ever go beyond them? Do physical objects come within its scope? Do the thoughts and feelings of others? Some philosophers have held that moral and aesthetic values can be objects of knowledge. Numbers and abstract entities have also been included. Indeed Plato seems to have thought that these were the only things that could be really known. Religious persons have claimed to be acquainted with a deity. And does not the experience of mystics suggest that the rays can penetrate beyond the actual world? But must there then not be a suprasensible reality? For it is taken for granted that whatever the searchlight can illuminate must in some manner exist.

Not all these questions are fictitious. There are genuine problems about the character and extent of what can be known. But this fashion of presenting them is a great impediment to their solution. It suggests that all that need be done to discover what it is possible to know, and consequently what is real, is to examine the states of mind of those who lay claim to knowledge. But, setting aside the question how such an examination could be made, it would be little to the purpose. The most that it could reveal would be that the subjects were having certain experiences and that they were convinced of the truth of whatever it was that these experiences led them to assert. But this would not prove that they knew anything at all, except, possibly, that they were having the experiences in question. It would still have to be established by an independent argument that the experiences disclosed the existence of anything beyond themselves. And there is another way in which this talk of knowing objects is misleading. It fosters mistaken views of the dependence of questions about the criteria of knowledge upon questions about reality. Thus followers of Plato are apt to make such pronouncements as that 'the perfectly real can alone be perfectly known':[1] but it is not clear even what this means unless it is merely a portentous way of saying that one cannot know what is not the case. We shall see, for example, that the fact

[1] Dean Inge, 'Philosophy and Religion', *Contemporary British Philosophy*, 1st series, p. 191.

that historical statements can be known does not oblige us to conclude that the past is real, unless to say that the past is real is just a way of saying that there are historical statements which are true. In this, as in other cases, it will be found that questions about the possibility of knowledge are to be construed as questions about the analysis of different types of statement and about the grounds that there may be for accepting them.

The mistaken doctrine that knowing is an infallible state of mind may have contributed to the view, which is sometimes held, that the only statements that it is possible to know are those that are themselves in some way infallible. The ground for this opinion is that if one knows something to be true one cannot be mistaken. As we remarked when contrasting knowledge with belief, it is inconsistent to say 'I know but I may be wrong'. But the reason why this is inconsistent is that saying 'I know' offers a guarantee which saying 'I may be wrong' withdraws. It does not follow that for a fact to be known it must be such that no one could be mistaken about it or such that it could not have been otherwise. It is doubtful if there are any facts about which no one could be mistaken, and while there are facts which could not be otherwise, they are not the only ones that can be known. But how can this second point be reconciled with the fact that what is known must be true? The answer is that the statement that what is known must be true is ambiguous. It may mean that it is necessary that if something is known it is true; or it may mean that if something is known, then it is a necessary truth. The first of these propositions is correct; it restates the linguistic fact that what is not true cannot properly be said to be known. But the second is in general false. It would follow from the first only if all truths were necessary, which is not the case. To put it another way, there is a necessary transition from being known to being true; but that is not to say that what is true, and known to be true, is necessary or certain in itself.

If we are not to be bound by ordinary usage, it is still open to us to make it a rule that only what is certain can be known. That is, we could decide, at least for the purposes of philosophical discourse, not to use the word 'know' except with the implication that what was known was necessarily true, or, perhaps, certain in some other sense. The consequence would be that we could still speak of knowing the truth of *a priori* statements, such as those of logic and pure mathematics; and if there were any empirical statements, such as those describing the content of one's present experience, that were certain in themselves, they too might be included: but most of what we now correctly claim to know would not be knowable, in this allegedly strict sense. This proposal is feasible, but it does not appear to have anything much to recommend it. It is not as if a statement by being necessary became incapable of being doubted. Every schoolboy knows that it is possible to be unsure about a mathematical truth. Whether there are any empirical statements which are in any important sense indubitable is, as we shall see, a matter of dispute: if there are any they belong to a very narrow class. It is, indeed, important philosophically to distinguish between necessary and empirical statements, and in dealing with empirical statements to distinguish between different types and degrees of evidence. But there are better ways of bringing out these distinctions than by tampering

C

with the meaning, or the application, of the verb 'to know'.

(iv)

Discussion of method : philosophy and language

We have now answered some of the questions which are raised by a philosophical enquiry into the nature of knowledge. It has been found that there is no very close resemblance between the different instances which are correctly described as instances of knowing, and in particular that to know something does not consist in being in some special state of mind. There are facts which we can be said to know intuitively, but these intuitions cannot be infallible. It has further been shown that the conception of objects of knowledge can be philosophically misleading, and that while there is a sense in which one cannot be mistaken if one knows that something is so, this does not imply that what one knows is itself necessary or indubitable. The whole discussion was introduced as an example of philosophic method. Let us therefore consider, for a moment, how these conclusions have in fact been reached.

An important part of our procedure has been to put these general questions about knowledge to the test of particular instances. Thus the proof that one can know an object, in the sense of being able to recognize it, without making any conscious judgement about it, is that it is possible to find examples of such recognition where there is no evidence that any judgement is made. The proof that knowing how to do something need not include the ability to give an account of the way in which it is done is just that there are many things which people know how to do without their being able to

give any such accounts. To discover that there need
be no difference, in respect of being sure, between
knowing and believing, we need only look at cases in
which it turns out that someone does not know what
he thought he knew. Very often the reason for this is
that what he thought he knew was false. Consequently,
he could not have known it, he only believed it. But
there is no suggestion that his mental state was different
from what it was supposed to be. Had what he
claimed to know been true he would, in these circumstances, have known it. In such cases we show
that what might be thought to be a necessary factor
in a given type of situation is really not necessary, by
finding examples in which it does not occur. This
is essentially a method of disproof: we cannot so
decisively show that a certain factor is necessary,
merely by finding examples in which it does occur;
we have to be able to see that its presence is logically
required by the fact that the situation is of the given
type. At the same time we may test the view that it
is so required by searching for counter-examples.
That none are forthcoming is at least an indication that
it is correct. There is a certain analogy here with
scientific reasoning, except that it is not so much a
matter, as in the scientific case, of discovering whether
there are any counter-examples as of deciding whether
there could be. The question is whether there is anything that we should be prepared to count as an
exception to the suggested rule. Thus the proof that
knowing, in the sense of 'knowing that', is always
knowledge of some truth is that it would not otherwise
be reckoned as knowledge. But it is not always so
clear whether or not we should be prepared to admit
exceptions. And one way of finding out is to examine

carefully whatever might appear to be a doubtful case.

It does not matter whether the examples taken are actual or imaginary. In either case we describe a situation in order to see how it should be classified. Or if there be no doubt as to its classification, we may redescribe it in such a way as to bring to light certain features of it which might otherwise be overlooked. The argument therefore depends upon considerations of language ; in the present instance upon the ways in which we use, or propose to use, the verb 'to know'. But this does not mean that it is an argument about words, in any trivial sense, or that it is especially tied to the English language. We are concerned with the work that the word 'know' does, not with the fact that it is this particular word that does it. It is for this reason that we can spare ourselves a sociological investigation into the ways in which people actually do use words. For it would not matter if the popular practice were different from what we took it to be, so long as we were clear about the uses that we ourselves were ascribing to the word in question. And in talking about these uses we are talking about the uses of any words in any language that are, or may be, used in the same way. It is therefore indifferent whether, in this manner of philosophizing, we represent ourselves as dealing with words or as dealing with facts. For our enquiry into the use of words can equally be regarded as an enquiry into the nature of the facts which they describe.

Although we have not been in any way concerned with setting up a formal system, the argument has also been developed by means of deductive logic. Thus the proof that no cognitive state of mind could be infallible depends upon the logical truism that if two states of affairs are distinct a statement which refers to only one of them does not entail anything about the other. If the statement that someone is apprehending, or intuiting, something is to be regarded purely as a description of his state of mind it cannot follow from it that what he apprehends is true. A similar argument was used by Hume to prove that knowledge of causal relations 'is not, in any instance, attained by reasonings *a priori*'.[1] 'The effect', he says, 'is totally different from the cause, and consequently can never be discovered in it.'[2] Or again, 'there is no object, which implies the existence of any other if we consider these objects in themselves, and never look beyond the idea which we form of them'.[3] As Hume puts them, these statements are not obviously tautological; but they become so when it is seen that what he is saying is that when two objects are distinct, they are distinct; and consequently that to assert the existence of either one of them is not necessarily to assert the existence of the other.

When they are formulated in this way such statements may seem too trivial to be worth making. But their consequences are important and easily overlooked. The proof of this is that many philosophers have in fact maintained that causality is a logical relation and that there can be infallible acts of knowing. To refute them satisfactorily, we may need to do more than merely point out the logical mistake. We may have to consider how they could have come to be misled, what are the arguments which seem to support their view, how these arguments are to be met. In general, it will be found that the points of logic on which philosophical theories turn are simple. How much of moral

[1] D. Hume, *An Enquiry Concerning Human Understanding*, Part I, section iv, para. 23.

[2] *Ibid*. Part I, section iv, para. 25.

[3] D. Hume, *A Treatise of Human Nature*, Book I, Part III, section vi.

theory, for example, is centred upon the truism, again remarked by Hume, that 'ought' is not implied by 'is', that there can be no deductive step from saying how things are to saying how they ought to be. What is difficult is to make the consequences of such truisms palatable, to discover and neutralize the motives which lead to their being denied. It is the fact that much philosophizing consists in persuasive work of this sort, the fact also that in all philosophy so much depends upon the way in which things are put, that gives point to the saying that philosophy is an exercise in rhetoric. But if this is to be said, it must be understood that the word 'rhetoric' is not to be taken, as it now very often is, in a pejorative sense.

It is not my purpose to give an exhaustive list of philosophical procedures. Those that I have described are typical and important, but they are not the only ones that will come within our notice. In particular, it will be seen that philosophers do not limit themselves to uncovering the criteria which we actually use in assessing different types of statement. They also question these criteria; they may even go so far as to deny their validity. In this way they come to put forward paradoxes such as that matter is unreal or that no one can ever really know what goes on in the mind of another. In themselves such statements may seem merely perverse: their philosophical importance comes out in the discussion of what lies behind them.

(v)

Knowing as having the right to be sure

The answers which we have found for the questions we have so far been discussing have not yet put us in

a position to give a complete account of what it is to
know that something is the case. The first requirement is that what is known should be true, but this
is not sufficient; not even if we add to it the further
condition that one must be completely sure of what one
knows. For it is possible to be completely sure of
something which is in fact true, but yet not to know it.
The circumstances may be such that one is not entitled
to be sure. For instance, a superstitious person who
had inadvertently walked under a ladder might be convinced as a result that he was about to suffer some mis-
fortune; and he might in fact be right. But it would
not be correct to say that he knew that this was going
to be so. He arrived at his belief by a process of
reasoning which would not be generally reliable; so,
although his prediction came true, it was not a case of
knowledge. Again, if someone were fully persuaded
of a mathematical proposition by a proof which could
be shown to be invalid, he would not, without further
evidence, be said to know the proposition, even though
it was true. But while it is not hard to find examples of
true and fully confident beliefs which in some ways fail
to meet the standards required for knowledge, it is not
at all easy to determine exactly what these standards are.

One way of trying to discover them would be to
consider what would count as satisfactory answers to
the question How do you know? Thus people may be
credited with knowing truths of mathematics or logic
if they are able to give a valid proof of them, or even if,
without themselves being able to set out such a proof,
they have obtained this information from someone who
can. Claims to know empirical statements may be
upheld by a reference to perception, or to memory, or
to testimony, or to historical records, or to scientific

laws. But such backing is not always strong enough for knowledge. Whether it is so or not depends upon the circumstances of the particular case. If I were asked how I knew that a physical object of a certain sort was in such and such a place, it would, in general, be a sufficient answer for me to say that I could see it ; but if my eyesight were bad and the light were dim, this answer might not be sufficient. Even though I was right, it might still be said that I did not really know that the object was there. If I have a poor memory and the event which I claim to remember is remote, my memory of it may still not amount to knowledge, even though in this instance it does not fail me. If a witness is unreliable, his unsupported evidence may not enable us to know that what he says is true, even in a case where we completely trust him and he is not in fact deceiving us. In a given instance it is possible to decide whether the backing is strong enough to justify a claim to knowledge. But to say in general how strong it has to be would require our drawing up a list of the conditions under which perception, or memory, or testimony, or other forms of evidence are reliable. And this would be a very complicated matter, if indeed it could be done at all.

Moreover, we cannot assume that, even in particular instances, an answer to the question How do you know ? will always be forthcoming. There may very well be cases in which one knows that something is so without its being possible to say how one knows it. I am not so much thinking now of claims to know facts of immediate experience, statements like 'I know that I feel pain', which raise problems of their own into which we shall enter later on.[1] In cases of this

[1] *Vide* Chapter II, section iv.

sort it may be argued that the question how one knows does not arise. But even when it clearly does arise, it may not find an answer. Suppose that someone were consistently successful in predicting events of a certain kind, events, let us say, which are not ordinarily thought to be predictable, like the results of a lottery. If his run of successes were sufficiently impressive, we might very well come to say that he knew which number would win, even though he did not reach this conclusion by any rational method, or indeed by any method at all. We might say that he knew it by intuition, but this would be to assert no more than that he did know it but that we could not say how. In the same way, if someone were consistently successful in reading the minds of others without having any of the usual sort of evidence, we might say that he knew these things telepathically. But in default of any further explanation this would come down to saying merely that he did know them, but not by any ordinary means. Words like 'intuition' and 'telepathy' are brought in just to disguise the fact that no explanation has been found.

But if we allow this sort of knowledge to be even theoretically possible, what becomes of the distinction between knowledge and true belief? How does our man who knows what the results of the lottery will be differ from one who only makes a series of lucky guesses? The answer is that, so far as the man himself is concerned, there need not be any difference. His procedure and his state of mind, when he is said to know what will happen, may be exactly the same as when it is said that he is only guessing. The difference is that to say that he knows is to concede to him the right to be sure, while to say that he is only guessing

is to withhold it. Whether we make this concession
will depend upon the view which we take of his performance. Normally we do not say that people know things
unless they have followed one of the accredited routes
to knowledge. If someone reaches a true conclusion
without appearing to have any adequate basis for it,
we are likely to say that he does not really know it.
But if he were repeatedly successful in a given domain,
we might very well come to say that he knew the facts
in question, even though we could not explain how he
knew them. We should grant him the right to be sure,
simply on the basis of his success. This is, indeed, a
point on which people's views might be expected to
differ. Not everyone would regard a successful run
of predictions, however long sustained, as being by
itself a sufficient backing for a claim to knowledge.
And here there can be no question of proving that this
attitude is mistaken. Where there are recognized
criteria for deciding when one has the right to be sure,
anyone who insists that their being satisfied is still not
enough for knowledge may be accused, for what the
charge is worth, of misusing the verb 'to know'. But
it is possible to find, or at any rate to devise, examples
which are not covered in this respect by any established
rule of usage. Whether they are to count as instances
of knowledge is then a question which we are left free
to decide.

It does not, however, matter very greatly which
decision we take. The main problem is to state and
assess the grounds on which these claims to knowledge
are made, to settle, as it were, the candidate's marks.
It is a relatively unimportant question what titles we
then bestow upon them. So long as we agree about
the marking, it is of no great consequence where we

draw the line between pass and failure, or between the different levels of distinction. If we choose to set a very high standard, we may find ourselves committed to saying that some of what ordinarily passes for knowledge ought rather to be described as probable opinion. And some critics will then take us to task for flouting ordinary usage. But the question is purely one of terminology. It is to be decided, if at all, on grounds of practical convenience.

One must not confuse this case, where the markings are agreed upon, and what is in dispute is only the bestowal of honours, with the case where it is the markings themselves that are put in question. For this second case is philosophically important, in a way in which the other is not. The sceptic who asserts that we do not know all that we think we know, or even perhaps that we do not strictly know anything at all, is not suggesting that we are mistaken when we conclude that the recognized criteria for knowing have been satisfied. Nor is he primarily concerned with getting us to revise our usage of the verb 'to know', any more than one who challenges our standards of value is trying to make us revise our usage of the word 'good'. The disagreement is about the application of the word, rather than its meaning. What the sceptic contends is that our markings are too high; that the grounds on which we are normally ready to concede the right to be sure are worth less than we think; he may even go so far as to say that they are not worth anything at all. The attack is directed, not against the way in which we apply our standards of proof, but against these standards themselves. It has, as we shall see, to be taken seriously because of the arguments by which it is supported.

I conclude then that the necessary and sufficient conditions for knowing that something is the case are first that what one is said to know be true, secondly that one be sure of it, and thirdly that one should have the right to be sure. This right may be earned in various ways ; but even if one could give a complete description of them it would be a mistake to try to build it into the definition of knowledge, just as it would be a mistake to try to incorporate our actual standards of goodness into a definition of good. And this being so, it turns out that the questions which philosophers raise about the possibility of knowledge are not all to be settled by discovering what knowledge is. For many of them reappear as questions about the legitimacy of the title to be sure. They need to be severally examined ; and this is the main concern of what is called the theory of knowledge.

CHAPTER II

SCEPTICISM AND CERTAINTY

(i)

Philosophical scepticism

I HAVE said that what the philosophical sceptic calls in question is not the way in which we apply our standards of proof, but these standards themselves. But not all questioning of accepted canons of evidence is philosophical. There was a time when people believed that examining the entrails of birds was a way of discovering whether a certain course of action would be propitious; whether, for example, the occasion was favourable for joining battle. Then any sceptic who doubted the value of such a method of divination would have been questioning an accepted canon of evidence. And it is now agreed that he would in fact have been right. But the justification for his doubt would have been not philosophical, but scientific. It might have been the case that these so-called omens were systematically connected with the events which they were supposed to presage : but experience shows otherwise. In the same way a mediaeval doubter might have raised the question whether the failure to survive a trial by ordeal was a trustworthy indication of guilt. He, too, would have been challenging a recognized method of proof; and his scepticism would have been justified. But, again, it would have been justified on scientific grounds. It is a matter of empirical fact that the innocent, no less than the guilty, are susceptible to physical injury and death.

The peculiarity of the philosopher's doubts is that they are not in this way connected with experience. Experience does indeed show that such reputed sources of knowledge as memory or perception or testimony are fallible. But the philosophical sceptic is not concerned, as a scientist would be, with distinguishing the conditions in which these sources are likely to fail from those in which they can normally be trusted. Whereas the enlightened thinker who casts doubt upon the reliability of omens is suggesting that they do not yield good enough results, that this method of prognostication does not reach a standard which other methods could, and perhaps do, satisfy, the philosophical sceptic makes no such distinction : his contention is that any inference from past to future is illegitimate. Similarly, he will maintain not merely that there are circumstances in which a man's senses are liable to deceive him, as when he is suffering from some physiological disorder, but rather that it is to be doubted whether the exercise of sense-perception can in any circumstances whatever afford proof of the existence of physical objects. He will argue not merely that memory is not always to be trusted, but that there is no warrant for supposing that it ever is : the doubt which he raises is whether we can ever be justified in inferring from present experiences to past events. In questioning one's right to believe in the experiences of others he will not be content with producing empirical evidence to show how easily one may be mistaken ; so far from encouraging us to be more circumspect, his argument is designed to show that however circumspect we are it makes no difference : it puts the thoughts and feelings of others behind a barrier which it is impossible that one should ever penetrate.

The fact that this type of scepticism is so undiscriminating in its scope, that it rains alike on the just and the unjust, has been thought to expose it to an easy refutation. Just as, to use a simile of Ryle's, 'there can be false coins only where there are coins made of the proper materials by the proper authorities',[1] so, it is argued, there can be times when our senses deceive us only if there are times when they do not. A perception is called illusory by contrast with other perceptions which are veridical: therefore to maintain that all perceptions must be illusory would be to deprive the word 'illusory' of its meaning. This rejoinder would not, indeed, be fatal to a more moderate sceptic who held, not that all perceptions are bound to be illusory, but only that we can never really know that any are not; but he too is exposed to a similar objection. For how, it may be asked, could we ever discover that any appearances were deceptive unless we knew that some were trustworthy? From a distance, or in a dim light, I may mistake the shape or colour of the thing that I am looking at; I may confuse one object with another; in exceptional conditions, I may even think that I am perceiving something when there is nothing there at all: but I should not know that I made these errors unless I were in a position to correct them. From close at hand and in a stronger light I can see what the colour and shape of the thing really are, and knowing this I am enabled to infer that I saw them wrongly before. I learn that I have had a hallucination because the further course of my experience assures me that the object which I thought I saw does not exist. In the same way, the only reason that I have for thinking that I suffer from errors of memory

[1] G. Ryle, *Dilemmas*, p. 95.

is that what I seem to remember sometimes runs counter to other historical evidence which I am entitled to accept : my only reason for supposing that I am wrong about the experiences of others is that I make judgements about them which are inconsistent with what I subsequently discover to be right.

This argument is not decisive. It is true that no judgements of perception would be specially open to distrust unless some were trustworthy ; but this is not a proof that we cannot be mistaken in trusting those that we do. Even granting that it makes no sense to say that all our perceptions are delusive, any one of them still may be. We have to make good our claim to know that some particular ones are not. And the same applies to the other types of judgement which the sceptic impugns. From the fact that our rejection of some of them is grounded on our acceptance of others it does not follow that those that we accept are true.

Nevertheless the argument does show that these general forms of scepticism can find no justification in experience. A historian who is distrustful of one of his authorities may have his suspicions confirmed by finding that the reports which this authority gives conflict with the evidence that is available from other sources ; if these sources are numerous and independent, and if they agree with one another, he will be reasonably confident that their account of the matter is correct. But if his doubts embraced every statement which referred to the past, there would be no such way of confirming them ; for all the relevant evidence would be equally suspect. In the same way, a scientist who is sceptical of the truth of some particular hypothesis may justify himself by showing that it is at variance with some well-established theory. But for someone who maintains that all inductive reasoning is illegitimate there are no well-established theories; there are theories which have not as yet been confuted, but they are not considered any more worthy of credence than those that have; nor, on this view, does the fact that a theory has been falsified make it any the less likely to hold good in future cases. It is, indeed, a matter of experience that general hypotheses do meet with counter-instances; and it might therefore seem that the view that all inductive reasoning is illegitimate had some empirical support. But this conclusion would be mistaken; or rather, it would misrepresent the sceptic's standpoint. His thesis is not that every theory, or hypothesis, will eventually break down, but that the accumulation of favourable instances, however long continued, affords us no good reason for believing it. And clearly the validity of this contention is independent of the actual course of our experience.

If experience cannot justify the sceptic, neither can it refute him. Psychologically, indeed, he may receive encouragement from the fact that by following our accepted standards of proof we sometimes arrive at beliefs which turn out to be false: it would be hard for him to get a hearing if the procedures which he questions never led us astray. But it is not essential to his position that this be so. All that he requires is that errors should be possible, not that they should actually occur. For his charge against our standards of proof is not that they work badly; he does not suggest that there are others which would work better. The ground on which he attacks them is that they are logically defective; or if not defective, at any rate logically questionable.

When we claim the right to be sure of the truth of

D

any given statement, the basis of the claim may be either that the statement is self-evident, or that its truth is directly warranted by our experience, or that it is validly derivable from some other statement, or set of statements, of which we have the right to be sure. Accordingly, if such claims are to be challenged, it may be argued either that the statements which we take as requiring no further proof, beyond an appeal to intuition or experience, are themselves not secure, or that the methods of derivation which we regard as valid may not really be so. These lines of argument do not exclude each other, and both have been pursued. It has been queried whether we can ever be in a position to say of any statement that there is no doubt about its truth ; and this query extends to the validity even of deductive reasoning : for if nothing is certain, then it is not certain that one statement follows from another. But our justification for deriving statements from one another is put in question chiefly in the cases where the transition is not deductive, or at least not obviously so.   There is, or has been thought to be, a general problem of induction which concerns the validity of all types of factual inference : but, as we have noted, there are also special problems concerning our right to pass from one sort of statement to another ; they raise such questions as whether, or how, we are justified in making assertions about physical objects on the basis of our sense-experiences, or in attributing experiences to others on the evidence of their behaviour, or in regarding our memories as giving us knowledge of the past.   It is by forcing us to consider questions of this sort that the sceptic performs his main service to philosophy.   But before attempting to examine them it may be well for us first to discuss the problem of certainty; the question whether there are any statements whose truth can be established beyond the possibility of doubt.

(ii)
The quest for certainty

The quest for certainty has played a considerable part in the history of philosophy : it has been assumed that without a basis of certainty all our claims to knowledge must be suspect. Unless some things are certain, it is held, nothing can be even probable. Unfortunately it has not been made clear exactly what is being sought. Sometimes the word 'certain' is used as a synonym for 'necessary' or for '*a priori*'. It is said, for example, that no empirical statements are certain, and what is meant by this is that they are not necessary in the way that *a priori* statements are, that they can all be denied without self-contradiction. Accordingly, some philosophers take *a priori* statements as their ideal. They wish, like Leibniz, to put all true statements on a level with those of formal logic or pure mathematics ; or, like the existentialists, they attach a tragic significance to the fact that this cannot be done. But it is perverse to see tragedy in what could not conceivably be otherwise ; and the fact that all empirical statements are contingent, that even when true they can be denied without self-contradiction, is itself a matter of necessity. If empirical statements had the formal validity which makes the truths of logic unassailable they could not do the work that we expect of them ; they would not be descriptive of anything that happens. In demanding for empirical statements the safeguard of logical necessity, these philosophers have failed to see that they would thereby rob them of their factual content.

Neither is this the only way in which their ideal of *a priori* statements fails them. Such statements are, indeed, unassailable, in the sense that, if they are true, there are no circumstances in which they could have been false. One may conceive of a world in which they had no useful application, but their being useless would not render them invalid : even if the physical processes of addition or subtraction could for some reason not be carried out, the laws of arithmetic would still hold good. But from the fact that *a priori* statements, if they are true, are unassailable in this sense, it does not follow that they are immune from doubt. For, as we have already remarked, it is possible to make mistakes in mathematics or in logic. It is possible to believe an *a priori* statement to be true when it is not. And we have seen that it is vain to look for an infallible state of intuition, which would provide a logical guarantee that no mistake was being made. Here too, it may be objected that the only reason that we have for concluding that any given *a priori* statement is false is that it contradicts some other which is true. That we can discover our errors shows that we have the power to correct them. The fact that we sometimes find ourselves to be mistaken in accepting an *a priori* statement, so far from lending favour to the suggestion that all those that we accept are false, is incompatible with it. But this still leaves it open for us to be at fault in any particular case. There is no special set of *a priori* statements of which it can be said that just these are beyond the reach of doubt. In very many instances the doubt would not, indeed, be serious. If the validity of some logical principle is put in question, one may be able to find a way of proving or disproving it. If it be suggested that the proof itself is suspect, one may obtain reassurance by going over it again. When one has gone over it again and satisfied oneself that there is nothing wrong with it, then to insist that it may still not be valid, that the conclusion may not really have been proved, is merely to pay lip-service to human fallibility. The doubt is maintained indefinitely, because nothing is going to count as its being resolved. And just for this reason it is not serious. But to say that it is not serious is not logically to exclude it. There can be doubt so long as there is the possibility of error. And there must be the possibility of error with respect to any statement, whether empirical or *a priori*, which is such that from the fact that someone takes it to be so it does not follow logically that it is so. We have established this point in our discussion of knowledge, and we have seen that it is not vitiated by the fact that in the case of *a priori* statements there may be no other ground for accepting them than that one sees them to be true.

Philosophers have looked to *a priori* statements for security because they have assumed that inasmuch as these statements may themselves be certain, in the sense of being necessary, they can be certainly known. As we have seen, it may even be maintained that only what is certainly true can be certainly known. But this, it must again be remarked, is a confusion. *A priori* statements can, indeed, be known, not because they are necessary but because they are true and because we may be entitled to feel no doubt about their truth. And the reason why we are entitled to feel no doubt about their truth may be that we can prove them, or even just that we can see them to be valid ; in either case there is an appeal to intuition, since we have at some point to claim to be able to see the validity of a proof. If the validity of every proof had to be proved in its turn, we should fall into an infinite regress. But to allow that there are times when we may justifiably claim the right to be sure of the truth of an *a priori* statement is not to allow that our intuitions are infallible. One is conceded the right to be sure when one is judged to have taken every reasonable step towards making sure : but this is still logically consistent with one's being in error. The discovery of the error refutes the claim to knowledge ; but it does not prove that the claim was not, in the circumstances, legitimately made. The claim to know an *a priori* statement is satisfied only if the statement is true ; but it is legitimate if it has the appropriate backing, which may, in certain cases, consist in nothing more than the statement's appearing to be self-evident. Even so, it may fail : but if such claims were legitimate only when there was no logical possibility of error, they could not properly be made at all.

Thus, if the quest for certainty is simply a quest for knowledge, if saying that a statement is known for certain amounts to no more than saying that it is known, it may find its object in *a priori* statements, though not indeed in them uniquely. If, on the other hand, it is a search for conditions which exclude not merely the fact, but even the possibility, of error, then knowledge of *a priori* statements does not satisfy it. In neither case is the fact that these *a priori* statements may themselves be certain, in the sense of being necessary, relevant to the issue. Or rather, as we have seen, it is relevant only if we arbitrarily decide to make it so.

(iii)
'*I think, therefore I am*'

The attempt to put knowledge on a foundation which would be impregnable to doubt is historically associated with the philosophy of Descartes. But Descartes, though he regarded mathematics as the paradigm of knowledge, was aware that its *a priori* truths are not indubitable, in the sense that he required. He allowed it to be possible that a malignant demon should deceive him even with respect to those matters of which he was the most certain.[1] The demon would so work upon his reason that he took false statements to be self-evidently true. The hypothesis of there being such an arch-deceiver is indeed empty, since his operations could never be detected : but it may be regarded as a picturesque way of expressing the fact that intuitive conviction is not a logical guarantee of truth. The question which Descartes then raises is whether, of all the propositions which we think we know, there can be any that escape the demon's reach.

His answer is that there is one such proposition : the famous *cogito*, *ergo sum* : I think, therefore I am.[2] The demon might perhaps have the power to make me doubt whether I was thinking, though it is difficult to see what this would come to ; it is not clear what such a state of doubt would be. But even allowing that the expression 'I am doubting whether I am thinking' describes a possible situation, the doubt must be unwarranted. However much he can shake my confidence, the demon cannot deceive me into believing that I am thinking when I am not. For if I believe that I am thinking, then I must believe truly, since my believing

---

[1] René Descartes, *Meditations on the First Philosophy*, Meditation I.
[2] *Vide* Meditation II and *Discourse on Method*, Part IV.

that I am thinking is itself a process of thought. Consequently, if I am thinking, it is indubitable that I am thinking, and if it is indubitable that I am thinking, then, Descartes argues, it is indubitable that I exist, at least during such times as I think.

Let us consider what this argument proves. In what sense is the proposition that I think, and consequently that I exist, shown to be indubitable ? It is not a question for psychology. The suggestion is not that it is physically impossible to doubt that one is thinking, but rather that it somehow involves a logical impossibility. Yet while there may be some question about the meaning that one should attach to the statement that I doubt whether I am thinking, it has not been shown to be self-contradictory. Nor is the statement that I am thinking itself the expression of a necessary truth. If it seems to be necessary, it is because of the absurdity of denying it. To say 'I am not thinking' is self-stultifying since if it is said intelligently it must be false : but it is not self-contradictory. The proof that it is not self-contradictory is that it might have been true. I am now thinking but I might easily not have been. And the same applies to the statement that I exist. It would be absurd for me to deny that I existed. If I say that I do not exist, it must be false. But it might not have been false. It is a fact that I exist, but not a necessary fact.

Thus neither 'I think' nor 'I exist' is a truth of logic : the logical truth is only that I exist if I think. And we have seen that even if they were truths of logic they would not for that reason be indubitable. What makes them indubitable is their satisfying a condition which Descartes himself does not make explicit, though his argument turns upon it. It is that their truth follows from their being doubted by the person who expresses them. The sense in which I cannot doubt the statement that I think is just that my doubting it entails its truth : and in the same sense I cannot doubt that I exist. There was therefore no need for Descartes to derive '*sum*' from '*cogito*'; for its certainty could be independently established by the same criterion.

But this certainty does not come to very much. If I start with the fact that I am doubting, I can validly draw the conclusion that I think and that I exist. That is to say, if there is such a person as myself, then there is such a person as myself, and if I think, I think. Neither does this apply only to me. It is obviously true of anyone at all that if he exists he exists and that if he thinks he thinks. What Descartes thought that he had shown was that the statements that he was conscious, and that he existed, were somehow privileged, that, for him at least, they were evidently true in a way which distinguished them from any other statements of fact. But this by no means follows from his argument. His argument does not prove that he, or anyone, knows anything. It simply makes the logical point that one sort of statement follows from another. It is of interest only as drawing attention to the fact that there are sentences which are used in such a way that if the person who employs them ever raises the question whether the statements which they express are true, the answer must be yes. But this does not show that these statements are in any way sacrosanct, considered in themselves.

Yet surely I can be certain that I am conscious, and that I exist. Surely my evidence for this could not be stronger than it is. But again it is not clear what is

being claimed when it is said that these things are
certain or that one can be certain of them. Perhaps
only that I know that they are so, and of course I do.
But these are not the only facts that I know, nor, as it
sometimes appears to be suggested, is my knowing
them a condition of my knowing anything else. It is
conceivable that I should not have been self-conscious,
which is to say that I should not know that I existed ;
but it would not follow that I could not know many
other statements to be true. In theory, I could know
any of the innumerable facts which are logically independent of the fact of my existing. I should indeed
know them without knowing that I knew them, though
not necessarily without knowing that they were known :
my whole conception of knowledge would be impersonal. Perhaps this is a strange supposition, but it
is not self-contradictory.

But while in the case of other facts which I may
reasonably claim to know, it is at least conceivable that
the evidence which I have for them should be even
stronger than it is, surely the fact that I exist and the
fact that I am conscious stand out for the reason that
in their case the evidence is perfect. How could I
possibly have better evidence than I do for believing
that I am conscious, let alone for believing that I
exist ? This question is indeed hard to answer, but
mainly because it seems improper in these cases to
speak of evidence at all. If someone were to ask me
How do you know that you are conscious ? What
evidence have you that you exist ? I should not know
how to answer him : I should not know what sort of
answer was expected. The question would appear to
be a joke, a parody of philosophical cautiousness. If it
were seriously pressed, I might become indignant :

What do you mean, how do I know that I exist? I am here, am I not, talking to you? If a 'philosophical' answer were insisted on, it might be said that I proved that I existed and that I was conscious by appealing to my experience. But not then to any particular experience. Any feeling or perception that I cared to instance would do equally well. When Hume looked for an impression of his self, he failed to find one : he always stumbled instead upon some particular perception.[1] He allowed that others might be luckier, but in this he was ironical. For the point is not that to have an experience of one's self is to perform a remarkably difficult feat of introspection : it is that there is nothing that would count as having an experience of one's self, that the expression 'having an experience of one's self' is one for which there is no use. This is not to say that people are not self-conscious, in the sense that they conceive of things as happening to themselves. It is that the consciousness of one's self is not one experience among others, not even, as some have thought, a special experience which accompanies all the others. And this is not a matter of psychology but of logic. It is a question of what self-consciousness is understood to mean.

If there is no distinctive experience of finding out that one is conscious, or that one exists, there is no experience at all of finding out that one is not conscious, or that one does not exist. And for this reason it is tempting to say that sentences like 'I exist', 'I am conscious', 'I know that I exist', 'I know that I am conscious' do not express genuine propositions. That Mr. A exists, or that Mr. A is conscious, is a genuine proposition ; but it may be argued that it is not what

[1] *A Treatise of Human Nature*, Book I, Part IV, section vi.

is expressed by 'I exist' or 'I am conscious', even
when I am Mr. A.   For although it be true that I am
Mr. A, it is not necessarily true.   The word 'I' is not
synonymous with 'Mr. A' even when it is used by
Mr. A to refer to himself.   That he is Mr. A, or that he
is identifiable in any other manner, is an empirical
statement which may be informative not only to others,
but also in certain circumstances to Mr. A himself, for
instance if he has lost his memory.   It cannot therefore be reasoned that because one may succeed in
expressing genuine propositions by replacing the 'I' in
such sentences as 'I am conscious' or 'I exist' by a
noun, or descriptive phrase, which denotes the person
concerned, these sentences still have a factual meaning
when this replacement is not made.

All the same it is not difficult to imagine circumstances in which they would have a use.   'I am
conscious' might be said informatively by someone
recovering from a swoon.   If I had been presumed to
be dead there might be a point in my proclaiming that
I still existed.   On recovering consciousness after some
accident or illness, I might make this remark even to
myself, and make it with a sense of discovery.   Just
as there are moments between sleep and waking when
one may seriously ask oneself if one is awake, so there
are states of semi-consciousness in which saying 'I
exist' answers a genuine question.   But what information does this answer give ?   If I have occasion to tell
others that I exist, the information which they receive
is that there exists a man answering to some description,
whatever description it may be that they identify me
by ;   it would not be the same in every case.   But when
I tell myself that I exist, I do not identify myself by
any description :   I do not identify myself at all.   The

information which I convey to myself is not that there exists a person of such and such a sort, information which might be false if I were mistaken about my own identity or character. Yet I am in fact a person of such and such a sort. There is nothing more to me than what can be discovered by listing the totality of the descriptions which I satisfy. This is merely an expression of the tautology that if a description is complete there is nothing left to be described. But can it not be asked what it is that one is describing ? The answer is that this question makes sense only as a request for further description : it implies that the description so far given is incomplete, as in fact it always will be. But then if, in saying that I exist, I am not saying anything about a description's being satisfied, what can I be saying ? Again it is tempting to answer that I am saying nothing.

Yet this would not be correct. Even when it is not doing duty for a description, nor coupled with one, the demonstrative 'I' may have a use. In the case which we envisaged, the case of a return to consciousness, it signals the presence of some experience or other. It does not, however, characterize this experience in any way. It merely points to the existence of whatever it is, in the given circumstances, that makes its own use possible. And since it is a contingent fact that any such situation does exist, the assertion which simply serves to mark it may be held to be informative. The sentence 'I exist', in this usage, may be allowed to express a statement which like other statements is capable of being either true or false. It differs, however, from most other statements in that if it is false it cannot actually be made. Consequently, no one who uses these words intelligently and correctly can use them to make a statement which he knows to be false. If he succeeds in making the statement, it must be true.

It is, therefore, a peculiar statement; and not only peculiar but degenerate. It is degenerate in the way that the statements which are expressed by such sentences as 'this exists' or 'this is occurring now' are degenerate. In all these cases the verbs which must be added to the demonstratives to make a grammatical sentence are sleeping partners. The work is all done by the demonstrative: that the situation, to which it points, exists, or is occurring, is a condition of the demonstrative's use. It is for this reason that any statement of this sort which is actually expressed must be true. It is not necessarily true, since the situation to which the demonstrative points might not have existed; it is logically possible that the condition for this particular use of the demonstrative should not have obtained. It is, however, like an analytic statement in that, once we understand the use of the demonstrative, here functioning as subject, the addition of the predicate tells us nothing further. Divorced from its context the whole statement has no meaning. Taken in context it is informative just as drawing attention to whatever it may be that the demonstrative is used to indicate. It approximates, therefore, to a gesture or to an ejaculation. To say 'I exist' or 'this is occurring now' is like saying 'look!' or pointing without words. The difference is that, in the formulation of the indicative sentence, the existential claim is made explicit; and it is because of this that the sentence may be said to express a statement, whereas the ejaculation or the gesture would not: one does not speak of ejaculations or gestures as being true or false. But there is no difference in the information conveyed.

Thus we see that the certainty of one's own existence is not, as some philosophers have supposed, the outcome of some primary intuition, an intuition which would have the distinctive property of guaranteeing the truth of the statement on which it was directed. It is indeed the case that if anyone claims to know that he exists, or that he is conscious, he is bound to be right. But this is not because he is then in some special state of mind which bestows this infallibility upon him. It is simply a consequence of the purely logical fact that if he is in any state whatever it follows that he exists; if he is any conscious state whatever it follows that he is conscious. He might exist without knowing it; he might even be conscious without knowing it, as is presumably the case with certain animals: there is at any rate no contradiction in supposing them to be conscious without supposing them to be conscious of themselves. But, as we have seen, if anyone does claim to know that he exists or that he is conscious, his claim must be valid, simply because its being valid is a condition of its being made. This is not to say, however, that he, or anyone, knows any description of himself, or his state of consciousness, to be true. To know that one exists is not, in this sense, to know anything about oneself any more than knowing that *this* exists is knowing anything about *this*. Knowing that I exist, knowing that this is here, is having the answer to a question which is put in such a form that it answers itself. The answer is meaningful only in its context, and in its context the condition of its being meaningful is its being true. This is the ground for saying that statements like 'I exist' are certain, but it is also the proof of their degeneracy: they have nothing

to say beyond what is implied in the fact that they
have a reference.

(iv)
Are any statements immune from doubt?

If our aim is never to succumb to falsehood, it would
be prudent for us to abstain from using language
altogether. Our behaviour might still be hesitant or
misguided but it is only with the use of language that
truth and error, certainty and uncertainty, come fully
upon the scene. It is only such things as statements or
propositions, or beliefs or opinions, which are expressible
in language, that are capable of being true or false,
certain or doubtful. Our experiences themselves are
neither certain nor uncertain ; they simply occur. It
is when we attempt to report them, to record or forecast
them, to devise theories to explain them, that we admit
the possibility of falling into error, or for that matter of
achieving truth. For the two go together : security
is sterile. It is recorded of the Greek philosopher
Cratylus that, having resolved never to make a statement of whose truth he could not be certain, he was in
the end reduced simply to wagging his finger. An
echo of his point of view is to be found in the disposition of some modern philosophers to regard the
expression of purely demonstrative statements like 'this
here now' as the ideal limit to which all narrative uses
of language should approach. It is a matter in either
case of gesticulating towards the facts without describing them. But it is just their failure to describe that
makes these gestures defective as a form of language.
Philosophers have been attracted by the idea of a
purely demonstrative use of words because they have

wanted to make the best of both worlds. They have sought as it were to merge their language with the facts it was supposed to picture ; to treat its signs as symbols, and yet bestow upon them the solidity which belongs to the facts themselves, the facts being simply there without any question of doubt or error arising. But these aims are incompatible. Purely demonstrative expressions are in their way secure ; but only because the information which they give is vanishingly small. They point to something that is going on, but they do not tell us what it is.

Some philosophers, however, have thought that they could go further than this. They have thought it possible to find a class of statements which would be both genuinely informative and at the same time logically immune from doubt. The statements usually chosen for this rôle contain a demonstrative component, but they are not wholly demonstrative ; they contain also a descriptive component which is supposed to characterize some present state of the speaker, or some present content of his experience. The sort of example that we are offered is 'I feel a headache' or 'this looks to me to be red' or 'this is louder than that', where 'this' and 'that' refer to sounds that I am actually hearing or, more ambitiously, 'it seems to me that this is a table' or 'I seem to remember that such and such an event occurred'. Such statements may be false as well as true : nor is their truth a condition of their being made. I may, for example, be lying when I say that I feel a headache. But while I may be lying and so deceive others, I cannot, so it is maintained, myself be in any doubt or in any way mistaken about the fact. I cannot be unsure whether I feel a headache, nor can I think that I feel a headache when I do not. And the same applies to the other examples. In all cases, so it is

E

alleged, if one misdescribes the nature of one's present experience, one must be doing so deliberately. One must be saying something which one knows for certain to be false.

Since the only way in which any statement of fact can be discovered either to be true or false is by someone's having some experience, these statements which are supposed, as it were, to photograph the details of our experiences seem to occupy a privileged position : for it would appear that it is their truth or falsehood that provides the test for the validity of all the others. For this reason they have sometimes been described as basic statements, or basic propositions. Or rather, it has been assumed that there must be some statements the recognition of whose truth or falsehood supplies the natural terminus to any process of empirical verification ; and statements which are descriptive of the present contents of experiences are selected as the most worthy candidates. The reason why they are so distinguished is that it is thought that they alone are directly and conclusively verifiable ; of all statements which have a descriptive content they alone are not subject to any further tests. If they were subject to further tests the process of verification would not terminate with them. But where else, then, could it terminate ? So these experiential statements, as we may call them, are taken as basic because they are held to be ' incorrigible '.

To say that these statements are incorrigible is not, however, to say that one's assessment of their truth or falsehood cannot ever be revised. Or if it does imply this, it is an error. Suppose that, feeling a headache, I write down in my diary the sentence ' I feel a headache '. To-morrow when I read this entry I may seem to remember that I did not make it seriously ; and so I may decide that the statement which it expressed was false. In the circumstances envisaged this decision would be wrong; but this does not mean that I am not free to make it, or to revise it in its turn. But, it may be said, the statement which you subsequently reject is not the same as the one you originally accepted. The statement which is expressed by the sentence 'I feel a headache now' is different from the statement which is expressed by the sentence 'I felt a headache then' even though the pronoun refers to the same person in each case and 'now' and 'then' refer to the same moment. Now there is indeed a sense in which these sentences do have different meanings; the correct translation of one of them into a different language would not be a correct translation of the other. Granted that their reference is the same, the difference in their form shows that they are uttered at different times. But I think it would be wrong to conclude that they expressed different statements; for the state of affairs which makes what is expressed by either of them true is one and the same. Moreover, it seems strange to say that when I verify a prediction about the course of my experience, the statement which I actually verify is different from the statement which embodies the prediction, since one is expressed by a sentence in the present and the other by a sentence in the future tense. Yet this would follow from the assumption that if two sentences differ in this way the statements which they express cannot be the same. I think, therefore, that this assumption is to be rejected, and consequently that experiential statements are not incorrigible in the sense that once they have been discovered to be true they cannot subsequently be denied. Clearly, if we have discovered them to be true, we shall be in error if we subsequently deny them: all that I am now maintaining is that it is an error which it is within our power to make.

But in what sense then is it at all plausible to claim that these statements are incorrigible ? Only, I think, in the sense that one's grounds for accepting them may be perfect. It is, therefore, misleading to talk of a class of incorrigible, or indubitable, statements as though 'being incorrigible' or 'being indubitable' were properties which belonged to statements in themselves. The suggestion is rather that there is a class of statements which in certain conditions only cannot be doubted ; statements which are known incorrigibly when they are made by the right person in the right circumstances and at the right time. Thus, in my view at least, the sentences 'he has a headache', when used by someone else to refer to me, 'I shall have a headache', used by me in the past with reference to this moment, and 'I have a headache' all express the same statement ; but the third of these sentences alone is used in such conditions as make it reasonable for me to claim that the statement is incorrigibly known. What is 'incorrigible' in this case is the strength of the basis on which I put the statement forward : not in the sense that the existence of such a basis cannot be denied or doubted by other persons, or by myself at other times, but that given its existence — and it is fundamental to the argument that I *am* given it — then, independently of all other evidence, the truth of the statement is perfectly assured. It is in this sense only that the statement may be regarded as not being subject to any further tests : a claim which may seem more modest when it is remarked that even if I am given a conclusive basis for accepting the truth of what I say in such conditions, the gift is immediately withdrawn. The conditions change; the experience is past; and I am left free to doubt or deny that I ever had it, and so again to put in question the truth of the statement which for a moment I 'incorrigibly' knew.

The ground, then, for maintaining that, while one is having an experience, one can know with absolute certainty the truth of a statement which does no more than describe the character of the experience in question is that there is no room here for anything short of knowledge: there is nothing for one to be uncertain or mistaken about. The vast majority of the statements which we ordinarily make assert more than is strictly contained in the experiences on which they are based: they would indeed be of little interest if they did not. For example, I am now seated in a vineyard: and I can fairly claim to know that there are clusters of grapes a few feet away from me. But in making even such a simple statement as 'that is a bunch of grapes', a statement so obvious that in ordinary conversation, as opposed, say, to an English lesson, it would never be made, I am in a manner going beyond my evidence. I can see the grapes: but it is requisite also that in the appropriate conditions I should be able to touch them. They are not real grapes if they are not tangible; and from the fact that I am having just these visual experiences, it would seem that nothing logically follows about what I can or cannot touch. Neither is it enough that I can see and touch the grapes: other people must be able to perceive them too. If I had reason to believe that no one else could, in the appropriate conditions, see or touch them, I should be justified in concluding that I was undergoing a hallucination. Thus, while my basis for making this assertion may be very strong, so strong indeed as to warrant a claim to knowledge, it is not conclusive; my experience, according to this argument, could still be what it is even though the grapes which I think that I am perceiving really do not exist. But suppose now that I make an even less ambitious statement: suppose that I assert merely that I am seeing what now looks to me to be a bunch of grapes, without the implication that there is anything really there at all; so that my statement would remain true even if I were dreaming or suffering a complete hallucination. How in that case could I possibly be wrong? What other people may experience, or what I myself may experience at other times, does not affect the issue. My statement is concerned only with what appears to me at this moment, and to me alone: whether others have the same impression is irrelevant. I may indeed be using words eccentrically. It may be that it is not correct in English to describe what I seem to be seeing as a bunch of grapes. But this, so it is argued, does not matter. Even if my use of words be unconventional, what I mean to express by them must be true.

(v)
Public and private uses of language

But this implies not only that the experience which I am describing is private, in the sense that it is mine and not anybody else's, but also that I am giving a private description of it. No doubt the words in which I express my statement are drawn from common speech. No doubt it can be understood by others as well as by myself: we have even allowed that it could be made by others, though they would not, like me, be qualified to make it incorrigibly. But if, provided

that I am not lying, my statement must be true however I express it, then even though I am using words
which belong to a public language, and using them
correctly, there is a sense in which my use of them is
private. It is private inasmuch as the meaning of my
words is supposed to be fixed entirely by the character
of the experience I am using them to indicate, independently of any public standard of usage. This
point may not have been made clear in our examples,
just because they have been chosen so as to be publicly
intelligible. For if I say that I am now seeing what
looks to me to be a bunch of grapes, the expression
'looks to me to be a bunch of grapes' may well be
understood to mean 'looks to me as a bunch of grapes
normally does look', not only to me but to any normal
observer; and in that case the question how it normally
looks is relevant to the truth of what I am saying. If I
were mistaken, as I might be, in supposing that the
standard appearance of a bunch of grapes was anything
like this, my statement would be false. But the
assumption is that my statement remains true even
though what I describe as looking like a bunch of
grapes does not by conventional standards merit this
description. And this means that I am using the
expression 'what looks to me to be a bunch of grapes'
simply to refer to the content of this experience, whatever it may be. This is not indeed how I normally
should use this expression, but it is the way in which
I am required to use it if my statement is to be incorrigible. In fact it is an expression which has a conventional use, but in so far as it serves merely to
characterize this momentary, private experience, any
other expression which I had chosen to invent for the
purpose would have done just as well. Its business

being merely to record an episode in my private history, no one else can be in a position to say that my use of it is incorrect.

At this point, however, some philosophers would object that this is not a possible use of language.[1] Whether or not the signs which I employ to record the ways things look to me have a conventional use, they must, if they are to function as descriptive symbols, be endowed with meaning: and they cannot be endowed with meaning unless they are used in accordance with a rule. But rules are public. There are objective tests for deciding whether they are being kept or broken. I can be right or wrong in saying that this looks to me like a bunch of grapes because I have ways of finding out how bunches of grapes are supposed to look: there is a public standard to which I can appeal. But if I do no more than affix an arbitrary label to some experience that I am having, I have no way of testing whether the label is correctly attached or not. There will, indeed, be no meaning in saying that its attachment is either correct or incorrect; and in that case it only masquerades as a label. It is not a symbol of anything at all. I am not bound to employ signs which are familiar to others: I can devise and use a private code. But though the materials of my language may be private, in the sense that only I employ them, its use cannot be: if it is to be a genuine language, it must function in the way that a public language does. It must be teachable to others whether or not it is ever actually taught: there must be means available to them as well as to me of deciding whether I observe

---

[1] *Vide* my symposium with R. Rhees, 'Can there be a Private Language?', *Supplementary Proceedings of the Aristotelian Society*, vol. xxviii.

its rules. But these conditions would not be met if my words served merely to label my experiences.

I do not think that this objection can be sustained. I shall not here discuss the more general question how far, and in what sense, one's private experiences are communicable; it will arise at a later stage when we come to consider the problems connected with one's knowledge of the minds of others.[1] For the present I wish only to maintain that whether or not my descriptions of my experiences are intelligible to others, their being so is not a condition of their being intelligible to myself. I agree that if I am to give my words a descriptive meaning, I must use them in accordance with some set of rules. My words must do more than simply point at my experiences : if a word applies to something it must apply to it not merely as being *this* but as being something of a certain sort. But it is not necessary that the question whether I keep or break my rules should be subject to a social check. Admittedly, if I cannot go beyond the sequence of my private feelings and impressions, if I am, as it were, in the position of one who is watching a cinema show with no power of identifying what he sees except by correlating one fleeting image with another, the means which I have for assuring myself that my use of words is consistent will be limited : I have in fact only my memory to rely on. And then it may be asked how the accuracy of my memory is itself to be tested. Only by comparing one memory with another. But is this a genuine test ? Am I not then, as Wittgenstein suggests, like a man who buys several copies of the morning paper in order to assure himself that what it says is true ?[2]

[1] *Vide* Chapter V, section iv.
[2] *Philosophical Investigations*, Part I, para. 265, p. 93.

But with any use of language the same difficulty arises. Suppose that I wish to make sure that I am employing the name of some colour correctly and that, not simply trusting to my memory, I consult a colour-atlas. To profit by it, I must be able to recognize the signs and samples which it contains. I must be able to see that such and such a mark upon the page is an inscription of the word I am concerned with; I must be able to tell whether such and such a colour which I am seeing or remembering is the same as the one with which the atlas links the word. If I have recourse to the testimony of others, I must be able to identify the shapes that they write down or the noises that they make. No doubt mistakes can always occur; but if one never accepted any identification without a further check, one would never identify anything at all. And then no descriptive use of language would be possible. But if one can recognize a word on a page, a sign made by some other person, the person himself and countless other objects, all without further ado, why should one not as immediately recognize one's own feelings and sensations? And why in that case should one not be able to describe them in accordance with certain rules of one's own? It would no doubt be an advantage if one's adherence to these rules were capable of being publicly checked, but it does not seem to be essential.

(vi)

Are mistakes about one's own immediate experience only verbal?

For those who have the use of language, there is an intimate connection between identifying an object and knowing what to call it. Indeed on many occasions one's recognizing whatever it may be is simply a matter of one's coming out with the appropriate word. Of course the word must be meant to designate the object in question, but there are not, or need not be, two separate processes, one of fixing the object and the other of labelling it. The intention is normally to be found in the way in which the label is put on. There is, however, a sense in which one can recognize an object without knowing how to describe it. One may be able to place the object as being of the same sort as such and such another, or as having appeared before on such and such occasions, although one forgets what it is called or even thinks that it is called something which it is not. To a certain extent this placing of the object is already a fashion of describing it : we are not now concerned with the cases where recognition, conceived in terms of adaptive behaviour, is independent of the use of any symbols at all : but our finding a description of this sort is consistent with our ignoring or infringing some relevant linguistic rule. And this can happen also when the rule is of one's own making, or at least constituted by one's own practice. When the usage which they infringe is private, such lapses can only be exceptional ; for unless one's practice were generally consistent, there would be no rule to break : but it is to be envisaged that they should now and then occur.

If this is so, one can be mistaken, after all, in the characterization of one's present experience. One can at least misdescribe it in the sense that one applies the wrong word to it ; wrong because it is not the word which by the rules of one's language is correlated with an 'object' of the sort in question. But the reply to

this may be that one would then be making only a
verbal mistake. One would be misusing words, but
not falling into any error of fact. Those who maintain
that statements which describe some feature of one's
present experience are incorrigible need not deny that
the sentences which express them may be incorrectly
formulated. What they are trying to exclude is the
possibility of one's being factually mistaken.

But what is supposed to be the difference in this
context between a verbal and a factual mistake ? The
first thing to remark is that we are dealing with words
which, though general in their application, are also
ostensive : that is, they are meant to stand for features
of what is directly given in experience. And with
respect to words of this kind, it is plausible to argue
that knowing what they mean is simply a matter of
being disposed to use them on the right occasions,
when these are presented. It then appears to follow
that to be in doubt as to the nature of something which
is given, to wonder, for example, what colour this looks
to me to be, is to be in doubt about the meaning of
a word. And, correspondingly, to misdescribe what is
given is to misuse a word. If I am not sure whether
this looks crimson, what I am doubting is whether
'crimson' is the right word to describe this colour : if
I resolve this doubt wrongly I have used the word
'crimson' when I should not or failed to use it when
I should. This example is made easier to accept
because the word 'crimson' has a conventional use. It
is harder to see how I can use a word improperly when
it is I alone who set the standard of propriety : my
mistake would then have to consist in the fact that I
had made an involuntary departure from some consistent practice which I had previously followed. In

any event, it is argued, my mistake is not factual. If I were to predict that something, not yet presented to me, was going to look crimson, I might very well be making a factual mistake. My use of the word 'crimson' may be quite correct. It properly expresses my expectation : only the expectation is not in fact fulfilled. But in such a case I venture beyond the description of my present experience : I issue a draft upon the facts which they may refuse to honour. But for them to frustrate me I must put myself in their power. And this it is alleged I fail to do when I am merely recording what is directly given to me. My mistakes then can only be verbal. Thus we see that the reason why it is held to be impossible to make a factual error in describing a feature of one's present experience is that there is nothing in these circumstances which is allowed to count as one's being factually mistaken.

Against this, some philosophers would argue that it is impossible to describe anything, even a momentary private experience, without venturing beyond it. If I say that what I seem to see is crimson, I am saying that it bears the appropriate resemblance in colour to certain other objects. If it does not so resemble them I have classified it wrongly, and in doing so I have made a factual mistake. But the answer to this is that merely from the statement that a given thing looks crimson, it cannot be deduced that anything else is coloured or even that anything else exists. The fact, if it be a fact, that the colour of the thing in question does not resemble that of other things which are properly described as crimson does indeed prove that in calling it crimson I am making a mistake ; I am breaking a rule which would not exist unless there were, or at any rate could be, other things to which the word applied. But in saying that this is crimson, I am not explicitly referring to these other things. In using a word according to a rule, whether rightly or wrongly, I am not talking about the rule. I operate it but I do not say how it operates. From the fact that I have to refer to other things in order to show that my description of something is correct, it does not follow that my description itself refers to them. We may admit that to describe is to classify; but this does not entail that in describing something one is bound to go beyond it, in the sense that one actually asserts that it is related to something else.

Let us allow, then, that there can be statements which refer only to the contents of one's present experiences. Then, if it is made a necessary condition for being factually mistaken that one should make some claim upon the facts which goes beyond the content of one's present experience, it will follow that even when these statements misdescribe what they refer to the error is not factual: and then there appears no choice but to say that it is verbal. The question is whether this ruling is to be accepted.

The assumption which lies behind it is that to understand the meaning of an ostensive word one must be able to pick out the instances to which it applies. If I pick out the wrong instances, or fail to pick out the right ones, I show that I have not learned how to use the word. If I hesitate whether to apply it to a given case, I show that I am so far uncertain of its meaning. Now there is clearly some truth in this assumption. We should certainly not say that someone knew the meaning of an ostensive word if he had no idea how to apply it; more than that, we require that his use of it should, in general, be both confident and right. But this is not to say that in every single case in which he hesitates over the application of the word, he must be in doubt about its meaning. Let us consider an example. Suppose that two lines of approximately the same length are drawn so that they both come within my field of vision and I am then asked to say whether either of them looks to me to be the longer, and if so which. I think I might very well be uncertain how to answer. But it seems very strange to say that what, in such a case, I should be uncertain about would be the meaning of the English expression 'looks longer than'. It is not at all like the case where I know which looks to me the longer, but having to reply in French, and speaking French badly, I hesitate whether to say 'plus longue' or 'plus large'. In this case I am uncertain only about the proper use of words, but in the other surely I am not. I know quite well how the words 'looks longer than' are used in English. It is just that in the present instance I am not sure whether, as a matter of fact, either of the lines does look to me to be longer than the other.

But if I can be in doubt about this matter of fact, I can presumably also come to the wrong decision. I can judge that this line looks to me to be longer than that one, when in fact it does not. This would indeed be a curious position to be in. Many would say that it was an impossible position, on the ground that there is no way of distinguishing between the way things look to someone and the way he judges that they look. After all he is the final authority on the way things look to him, and what criterion is there for deciding how things look to him except the way that he assesses them? But in allowing that he may be uncertain how a thing looks to him, we have already admitted this distinction. We have drawn a line between the facts and his assessment, or description, of them.[1] Even so, it may be objected, there is no sense in talking of there being a mistake unless it is at least possible that the mistake should be discovered. And how could it ever be discovered that one had made a mistake in one's account of some momentary, private experience ? Clearly no direct test is possible. The experience is past : it cannot be produced for re-inspection. But there may still be indirect evidence which would carry weight. To return to our example, if I look at the lines again, it may seem quite clear to me that A looks longer than B, whereas I had previously been inclined to think that B looked longer than A, or that they looked the same length. This does not prove that I was wrong before : it may be that they look to me differently now from the way they did then. But I might have indirect, say physiological, evidence that their appearance, that is the appearance that they offer to me, has not changed. Or I may have reason to believe that in the relevant conditions things look the same to certain other people as they do to me : and then the fact that the report given by these other people disagrees with mine may have some tendency to show that I am making a mistake. In any event it is common ground that one can misdescribe one's experience. The question is only whether such misdescription is always to be taken as an instance of a verbal mistake. My contention is that there are cases in which it is more plausible to say that the mistake is factual.

If I am right, there is then no class of descriptive

---

[1] Yes, but it may still be argued that his assessment, when he reaches it, *settles* the question. The point is whether a meaning can be given to saying that he decides wrongly. I suggest that it can.

statements which are incorrigible. However strong the experiential basis on which a descriptive statement is put forward, the possibility of its falsehood is not excluded. Statements which do no more than describe the content of a momentary, private experience achieve the greatest security because they run the smallest risk. But they do run some risk, however small, and because of this they too can come to grief. Complete security is attained only by statements like 'I exist' which function as gesticulations. But the price which they pay for it is the sacrifice of descriptive content.

We are left still with the argument that some statements must be incorrigible, if any are ever to be verified. If the statements which have been taken as basic are fallible like all the rest, where does the process of verification terminate? The answer is that it terminates in someone's having some experience, and in his accepting the truth of some statement which describes it, or, more commonly, the truth of some more far-reaching statement which the occurrence of the experience supports. There is nothing fallible about the experience itself. What may be wrong is only one's identification of it. If an experience has been misidentified, one will be misled into thinking that some statement has been verified when it has not. But this does not mean that we never verify anything. There is no reason to doubt that the vast majority of our experiences are taken by us to be what they are; in which case they do verify the statements which are construed as describing them. What we do not, and cannot, have is a logical guarantee that our acceptance of a statement is not mistaken. It is chiefly the belief that we need such a guarantee that has led philosophers to hold that some at least of the statements which refer

F

to what is immediately given to us in experience must be incorrigible. But, as I have already remarked, even if there could be such incorrigible statements, the guarantee which they provided would not be worth very much. In any given case it would operate only for a single person and only for the fleeting moment at which he was having the experience in question. It would not, therefore, be of any help to us in making lasting additions to our stock of knowledge.

In allowing that the descriptions which people give of their experiences may be factually mistaken, we are dissociating having an experience from knowing that one has it. To know that one is having whatever experience it may be, one must not only have it but also be able to identify it correctly, and there is no necessary transition from one to the other; not to speak of the cases when we do not identify our experiences at all, we may identify them wrongly. Once again, this does not mean that we never know, or never really know, what experiences we are having. On the contrary it is exceptional for us not to know. All that is required is that we should be able to give an account of our experiences which is both confident and correct; and these conditions are very frequently fulfilled. It is no rebuttal of our claim to knowledge that, in this as in other domains, it may sometimes happen that we think we know when we do not.

The upshot of our argument is that the philosopher's ideal of certainty has no application. Except in the cases where the truth of a statement is a condition of its being made, it can never in any circumstances be logically impossible that one should take a statement to be true when it is false; and this holds good whatever the statement may be, whether, for example, it is itself necessary or contingent. It would, however, be a mistake to express this conclusion by saying, lugubriously or in triumph, that nothing is really certain. There are a great many statements the truth of which we rightly do not doubt ; and it is perfectly correct to say that they are certain. We should not be bullied by the sceptic into renouncing an expression for which we have a legitimate use. Not that the sceptic's argument is fallacious ; as usual his logic is impeccable. But his victory is empty. He robs us of certainty only by so defining it as to make it certain that it cannot be obtained.

(vii)
How do we know ?

One reason why it is plausible to maintain that statements which do no more than describe the contents of present experiences are incorrigible is that we are not required to vindicate our claims to know that they are true. It would seem absurd to ask someone how he knew that he was in pain or how he knew that what he was seeing looked to him to be of such and such a colour. For what better answer could he give than that these just were the experiences that he was having ? This is not to say that there can not be independent evidence for the truth of such statements. Without it people other than the speaker would have no reason for accepting them, neither would he himself at other times. In certain cases, as we have seen, he may even use it to check the accuracy of his description of some present experience. But so long as he is actually having the experience in question, the independent evidence that there may be for its existence plays for him a subordinate rôle. His claim to know what the experience is, though it is subject to correction, is not considered to be in need of any external support.

In the ordinary way, however, the statements of fact which we claim to know are not limited to the description of our present experiences. If they refer to them at all they also refer beyond them, and in most instances they do not ostensibly refer to them at all. Even in the case of these statements we may not always be able to say how we know that they are true, but at least it is always pertinent to put the question; if no answer is obtained, the claim to knowledge becomes suspect, though it may still be upheld. To give an answer is to put forward some other statement which supports the statement of which knowledge is claimed; it is implied that this second statement is itself known to be true. Again, it may be asked how this is known, and then a third assertion may be made which supports the second. And so the process may continue until we reach a statement which we are willing to accept without a further reason. Not that it is theoretically impossible that a further reason should be found. It is just that at a certain point we decide that no further reason is required.

Thus, to ask how a statement is known to be true is to ask what grounds there are for accepting it. The question is satisfactorily answered if the grounds themselves are solid and if they provide the statement with adequate support. But here a distinction must be drawn between asking what grounds there are for accepting a given statement and asking what grounds a particular person actually has for accepting it. For example, if I am asked how I know that the earth is round, I may reply by giving the scientific evidence;

in so doing I shall probably not refer to any experiences that I myself have had. But the question may also be interpreted as asking not so much how this is known as how *I* know it : and if I construe it in this way my reply will take a different form. I may mention some source from which I derived the information, some book that I have read, or some person who has instructed me ; I may perhaps be able to add that I have myself made some of the relevant observations, such as that of watching a ship disappear over the horizon. It may well be, however, that I cannot now recall any particular occasion on which I was informed that the earth was round, or any particular observations that I have made which go to prove it. Yet I may still say that I know this to be so, on the ground that it is common knowledge. My personal licence for the statement may be lost, but by consulting the right authorities, or by carrying out certain experiments, I can easily get it renewed. In this case, as in a great many others, I answer the question how I know by referring not to experiences that I have actually had but rather to experiences that I could have if I chose.

Since nothing is known unless somebody knows it, there is a ground for saying that the first type of answer to the question 'How do you know?' reduces to the second. Having justified a claim to knowledge by testing the scientific, or historical, evidence, one may then be asked how these supporting statements themselves are warranted. If the question is pressed far enough, it seems that the answer must at some point take the form of saying that someone has actually observed whatever it may be. Further, since it is my claim that is being challenged, must I not end by referring, not just to observations that have been made

by someone or other, but to experiences of my own ?
But here, as we have just seen, this second type of
answer reverts to the first. For it will seldom be the
case that the appropriate reference is to any particular
experience that I either am, or remember, having.
Nearly always, it will be a matter of claiming that I
should have certain experiences if I took the proper
steps. But here the point of saying that I should have
these experiences is just that the facts are so ; in other
words, that the statements which they would verify are
true. It may be held even that these two claims are
equivalent, on the ground that every statement of fact
is ultimately reducible to statements about possible, if
not actual, experiences. Whether this is so or not is
a question into which we shall have to enter later on.

However this may be, it is clear that when, as is
commonly the case, a statement is accredited on the
basis of certain others, their support of it must be
genuine ; the passage from evidence to conclusion
must be legitimate. And it is at this point that the
sceptic attacks. He produces arguments to show that
the steps which we presume to be legitimate are not so
at all. It will be found that most of our claims to knowledge are thereby put in question, and not merely our
claims to knowledge but even our claims to rational
belief.

(viii)

Doubts about factual reasoning : the problem
of induction

The range of this scepticism varies. It may be applied
to all proof whatsoever or, somewhat less generally, only
to all forms of experimental proof. In the second case

it gives rise to the notorious problem of induction. This problem can be set out very simply. Inductive reasoning is taken to cover all the cases in which we pass from a particular statement of fact, or set of particular statements of fact, to a factual conclusion which they do not formally entail. The inference may be from particular instances to a general law, or proceed directly by analogy from one particular instance to another. In all such reasoning we make the assumption that there is a measure of uniformity in nature; or, roughly speaking, that the future will, in the appropriate respects, resemble the past. We think ourselves entitled to treat the instances which we have been able to examine as reliable guides to those that we have not. But, as Hume pointed out, this assumption is not demonstrable; the denial that nature is uniform, to whatever degree may be in question, is not self-contradictory. Neither, as Hume also saw, is there any means of showing, without logical circularity, that the assumption is even probable. For the only way of showing that it was probable would be to produce evidence which confirmed it, and it is only if there are fair samples in nature that any evidence can be confirmatory. But whether there are fair samples in nature is just the point at issue. The same considerations apply if we seek to justify some more specific hypothesis, or would-be law of nature. Unless it is treated as a definition, in which case the problem is merely transferred to that of making sure that the definition is ever satisfied, such a proposition will not be demonstrable; the denial of it will not be self-contradictory. And once again the arguments which are meant to show that it is probable will themselves invoke the assumption that inductive reasoning is to be relied on. There are those, indeed, who think that this difficulty can be circumvented by basing their assessments of the probability of hypotheses on an *a priori* theory of probability: and much ingenious work has been done towards this end. It seems to me, however, that it has been done in vain. For the *a priori* theory of probability is just a mathematical calculus of chances. And I do not see how from a purely formal calculus it is possible to derive any conclusion at all about what is in fact likely to happen. The calculus can indeed be used in conjunction with empirical premises: but then the justification of these empirical premises brings back the very difficulties that the appeal to the *a priori* calculus was intended to avoid.

For the most part, attempts to solve the problem of induction have taken the form of trying to fit inductive arguments into a deductive mould. The hope has been, if not to turn problematic inference into formal demonstration, at least to make it formally demonstrable that the premises of an inductive argument can in many cases confer a high degree of probability upon its conclusion. It has been thought that this could be achieved by bringing in additional premises about the constitution of the world. Logically the selection of these principles involves considerable difficulties ; merely to invoke the uniformity of nature, or a law of universal causation, will not be enough. But even if we suppose the logical requirements to be somehow met, it seems clear that this enterprise must fail. For if these principles are to do the work that is expected of them, they must themselves be empirical hypotheses ; and so once again the original problem returns with the question how they are to be justified.

Some philosophers of science attempt to rule out

these questions altogether by saying that they arise out of a misconception of scientific method. In their view, scientists do not employ inductive reasoning; or rather, in so far as they do employ it, it is only one of the means by which they arrive at their hypotheses; they are not, or do not need to be, concerned with its validity. For what matters to them is the worth of the hypothesis itself, not the way in which it has come to be believed. And the process of testing hypotheses is deductive. The consequences which are deduced from them are subjected to empirical verification. If the result is favourable the hypothesis is retained; if not, it is modified or rejected and another one adopted in its place. But even if this is the correct account of scientific method, it does not eliminate the problem of induction. For what would be the point of testing a hypothesis except to confirm it? Why should a hypothesis which has failed the test be discarded unless this shows it to be unreliable; that is, except on the assumption that having failed once it is likely to fail again? It is true that there would be a contradiction in holding both that a hypothesis had been falsified and that it was universally valid: but there would be no contradiction in holding that a hypothesis which had been falsified was the more likely to hold good in future cases. Falsification might be regarded as a sort of infantile disease which even the healthiest hypotheses could be depended on to catch. Once they had had it there would be a smaller chance of their catching it again. But this is not in fact the view that we take. So far from approaching nature in the spirit of those gamblers at roulette who see in a long run of one colour a reason for betting on the other, we assume in general that the longer a run has been the more it is likely to continue. But how is this assumption to be justified ? If this question could be answered, the problem of induction would be solved.

It does not seem, however, that it can be answered. What is demanded is a proof that what we regard as rational procedure really is so ; that our conception of what constitutes good evidence is right. But of what kind is this proof supposed to be ? A purely formal proof would not be applicable, and anything else is going to beg the question. For instance, it is often said that the ground for trusting scientific methods is simply that they work ; the predictions which they lead us to make most commonly turn out to be true. But the fact is only that they have worked up to now. To say that they work is, in this context, to imply that they will go on working in the future. It is tacitly to assume that the future can in this matter be relied on to resemble the past. No doubt this assumption is correct, but there can be no way of proving it without its being presupposed. So, if circular proofs are not to count, there can be no proof. And the same applies to any other assumption which might be used to guarantee the reliability of inductive reasoning. A proof which is formally correct will not do the work, and a proof which does the work will not be formally correct.

This does not mean that the use of scientific method is irrational. It could be irrational only if there were a standard of rationality which it failed to meet ; whereas in fact it goes to set the standard : arguments are judged to be rational or irrational by reference to it. Neither does it follow that specific theories or hypotheses cannot be justified. The justification of a hypothesis is to be found in the evidence which favours it. But if someone chooses to deny that the fact that a hypothesis has been so favoured is a ground for continuing to trust it, he cannot be refuted ; or rather he can be refuted only by reference to the standards which he questions, or rejects. No proof that we are right can be forthcoming : for at this stage nothing is going to be allowed to count as such a proof.

Thus, here again the sceptic makes his point. There is no flaw in his logic : his demand for justification is such that it is necessarily true that it cannot be met. But here again it is a bloodless victory. When it is understood that there logically could be no court of superior jurisdiction, it hardly seems troubling that inductive reasoning should be left, as it were, to act as judge in its own cause. The sceptic's merit is that he forces us to see that this must be so.

(ix)

The pattern of sceptical arguments

There is, however, a special class of cases in which the problems created by the sceptic's logic are not so easily set aside. They are those in which the attack is directed, not against factual inference as such, but against some particular forms of it in which we appear to end with statements of a different category from those with which we began. Thus doubt is thrown on the validity of our belief in the existence of physical objects, or scientific entities, or the minds of others, or the past, by an argument which seeks to show that it depends in each case upon an illegitimate inference. What is respectively put in question is our right to make the transition from sense-experiences to physical objects, from the world of common sense to the entities of science, from the overt behaviour of other people to their inner thoughts and feelings, from present to past. These are distinct problems, but the pattern of the sceptic's argument is the same in every case.

The first step is to insist that we depend entirely on the premises for our knowledge of the conclusion. Thus, it is maintained that we have no access to physical objects otherwise than through the contents of our sense-experiences, which themselves are not physical : we infer the existence of scientific entities, such as atoms and electrons, only from their alleged effects : another person's mind is revealed to us only through the state of his body or by the things he says and does : the past is known only from records or through our memories, the contents of which themselves belong to the present. Relatively to our knowledge of the evidence, our knowledge of the conclusion must in every case be indirect : and logically this could not be otherwise.

The second step in the argument is to show that the relation between premises and conclusion is not deductive. There can be no description of our sense-experiences, however long and detailed, from which it follows that a physical object exists. Statements about scientific entities are not formally deducible from any set of statements about their effects, nor do statements about a person's inner thoughts and feelings logically follow from statements about their outward manifestations. However strong the present evidence for the existence of certain past events may be, it is not demonstrative. There would be no formal contradiction in admitting the existence of our memory-experiences, or of any other of the sources of our knowledge of the past, and yet denying that the corresponding past events had ever taken place.

But then, the argument proceeds, these inferences are not inductive either. Assuming inductive inference to be legitimate at all, it carries us, to use a phrase of Hume's, from instances of which we have experience to those of which we have none.[1] But here it is essential that these instances of which we in fact have no experience should be such as we are capable of experiencing. Let it be granted, in spite of the problem of induction, that on the basis of what we do experience we are sometimes entitled to infer the existence of unobserved events : our reliance on argument will then be a substitute for the direct observations which, for some practical reason, we are unable to make. The position is quite different when the things whose existence we are claiming to infer not merely are not given to us in experience but never could be. For what foundation could there be in such a case for our inductive arguments and how could their success be tested ? Some philosophers even consider it to be nonsensical to assert the existence of an object which could not, at least in principle, be observed ; and clearly no amount of inductive evidence can warrant a meaningless conclusion. But even if one does not go so far as to call such conclusions meaningless, it must be admitted, according to this argument, that they can have no inductive backing. Experimental reasoning can carry us forward at a given level ; on the basis of certain sense-experiences it allows us to predict the occurrence of other sense-experiences ; from observations of the way a person is behaving it allows us to infer that his future behaviour will take such and

[1] *A Treatise of Human Nature*, Book I, Part III.

such a course. What it does not permit us is to jump from one level to another; to pass from premises concerning the contents of our sense-experiences to conclusions about physical objects, from premises concerning other people's overt behaviour to conclusions about their minds.

The last step is to argue that since these inferences cannot be justified either deductively or inductively, they cannot be justified at all. We are not entitled even to make the elementary move of inferring from our present experiences to the existence of past events, or, admitting the whole range of our experiences, to arrive at the existence of physical objects: and assuming that we had sufficient warrant for believing in the existence of the physical objects which make up the world of common sense, we still should not be entitled to make the transition from these to the entities of science, or from any physical phenomena to the existence of other minds. It would indeed be hard to find even a philosopher who was willing to accept these consequences. It is scarcely to be imagined that anyone should seriously maintain that we had no right whatsoever to be sure, or even moderately confident, of anything concerning physical objects, or the minds of others, or the past. But even if he shrinks from carrying his argument to what appears to be its logical conclusion, the sceptic may still insist that it presents a question for us to answer. No doubt we do know what he says we cannot know; we are at least called upon to explain how it is possible that we should.

The problem which is presented in all these cases is that of establishing our right to make what appears to be a special sort of advance beyond our data. The

level of what, for the purposes of the problem, we take
to be data varies ; but in every instance they are supposed to fall short, in an uncompromising fashion, of
the conclusion to which we look to them to lead us.
For those who wish to vindicate our claim to knowledge,
the difficulty is to find a way of bridging or abolishing
this gap.

Concern with the theory of knowledge is very much
a matter of taking this difficulty seriously. The different
ways of trying to meet it mark out different schools of
philosophy, or different methods of attacking philosophical questions. Apart from the purely sceptical
position, which sets the problem, there are four main
lines of approach. It is interesting that each of them
consists in denying a different step in the sceptic's
argument.

First, Naïve Realism. The naïve realist denies the
first step of all. He will not allow that our knowledge
of the various things which the sceptic wishes to put
beyond our reach is necessarily indirect. His position
is that the physical objects which we commonly perceive are, in a sense to be explained, directly ' given ' to
us, that it is not inconceivable that such things as
atoms and electrons should also be directly perceived,
that at least in certain favourable instances one can
inspect the minds of others, that memory makes us
directly acquainted with the past. The general attitude
displayed is that of intuitionism. It is in the same
spirit that philosophers maintain that they intuit moral
values, or try to justify induction by claiming the
power of apprehending necessary connections between
events. But of course it is possible to take up the
naïve realist's position on any one of these questions,
without being committed to it on the others.

Secondly, Reductionism. The reductionist allows the first step in the sceptic's argument, but denies the second. Although his philosophical temper is diametrically opposed to that of the naïve realist, or indeed to intuitionism in any form, they have this much in common. Both of them try to close the gap which the sceptic relies on keeping open. But whereas the naïve realist does so by bringing the evidence up to the conclusion, the reductionist's policy is to bring the conclusion down to the level of the evidence. His view, which we shall presently examine, is that physical objects are logically constructed out of the contents of our sense-experiences, just as the entities of science are nothing over and above their so-called effects. In the same way, he holds that statements which appear to be about the minds of others are equivalent to statements about their physical manifestations, and that statements which appear to be about the past are equivalent to statements about what are ordinarily regarded as records of the past, that is to statements about the present and future. Thus the conclusion, being brought down to the level of the evidence, is presented in every case as being deducible from it. It is again to be noted that one may take a reductionist view of any one of these questions without being bound to apply it to the others.

Thirdly, we have what may be called the Scientific Approach. This is the position of those who admit the first two steps in the sceptic's argument but deny the third. Unlike their predecessors, they accept the existence of the gap between evidence and conclusion, but they hold that it can be bridged by a legitimate process of inductive reasoning. Thus they will maintain that physical objects, though not directly observable in the way the naïve realists suppose, can be known to us indirectly as the causes of our sensations, just as the existence of scientific entities can be inferred from their effects, without our having to identify the two. On this view, the deliverances of memory, and other records, make the existence of the past an overwhelmingly probable hypothesis. Knowing that we ourselves have inner thoughts and feelings, we can attribute them to others by analogy.

Finally, there is the method of Descriptive Analysis. Here one does not contest the premises of the sceptic's argument, but only its conclusion. No attempt is made either to close or to bridge the gap : we are simply to take it in our stride. It is admitted that the inferences which are put in question are not deductive and also that they are not inductive, in the generally accepted sense. But this, it is held, does not condemn them. They are what they are, and none the worse for that. Moreover, they can be analysed. We can, for example, show in what conditions we feel confident in attributing certain experiences to others we can ; evaluate different types of record ; we can distinguish the cases in which our memories or perceptions are taken to be reliable from those in which they are not. In short, we can give an account of the procedures that we actually follow. But no justification of these procedures is necessary or possible. One may be called upon to justify a particular conclusion, and then one can appeal to the appropriate evidence. But no more in these cases than in the case of the more general problem of induction can there be a proof that what we take to be good evidence really is so. And if there cannot be a proof, it is not sensible to demand one. The sceptic's problems are insoluble because they are fictitious.

G

(x)

Remarks on the different methods of answering the sceptic

I do not wish to say, at this stage, that any one of these approaches is, or is not, correct. If any such judgement can be made, it must follow an examination of the various problems. Except that we shall not enter into the philosophy of science, we shall deal with each of them in detail. Though we have seen that they exhibit a common pattern, there are sufficient differences between them for it to be by no means certain that a single type of answer will be appropriate in every case: we may find that a method which works well in one instance works badly in another. Again, this is a matter for particular investigation. There are, however, one or two general remarks which it may be useful to make before we enter into the details of our enquiry.

First, as to naïve realism. The strength of the naïve realist lies in his allegiance to common sense. What he knows, he knows; the arguments which go to show that he may not know it after all do not affect him; by denying the first of the sceptic's premises he absolves himself from considering the rest. Neither will he allow any tampering with the subject-matter of his knowledge. Physical objects are physical objects, minds are minds, the past is the past. But while such truisms may be a useful corrective to the extravagances of more imaginative philosophers, they are not philosophically enlightening. In this, as in other fields, the failing of intuitionism is that it offers us no account of the way in which things are known. It may seem to offer an account, but the account is spurious. For to say that something is known by intuition or, as the naïve realist might put it, by direct acquaintance, is not at all to say *how* it is known. The addition of the explanatory phrase serves only to deny an explanation. It is justified only in the cases, if there are any, where no answer to the question how one knows is to be expected.

If the naïve realist tends to be too plain a man, the reductionist is hardly plain enough. Being willing to follow his arguments wherever they lead, he is not deterred by any appearance of paradox. To identify such things as atoms and electrons or, in another field, unconscious mental processes, with their alleged effects is not, indeed, unduly paradoxical : and perhaps the same can be said of the reduction of physical objects, like chairs and tables, to the contents of our sense-experiences, though here already there may be a protest on the part of common sense. But to maintain that when we appear to be speaking about the minds of others we are really speaking only about their bodies will seem to most people to be obviously false : while the view that all apparent references to the past are really references to the present, or future, is on the face of it preposterous. It is to be noted, however, that the reductionist does not embrace these paradoxes for their own sakes. He is convinced by argument that unless statements about the past, or physical objects, or the minds of others, are construed in this way, we can have no reason whatsoever for believing them to be true. He therefore accepts these analyses as the only alternative to outright scepticism. Since the consequences are so strange, one may suspect that there is something wrong with the argument. But even if the reductionist can be refuted, his errors are instructive. He takes us on a philosophical journey while the naïve realist, secure in the possession of his property, is content to stay at home.

The scientific approach, as I have called it, is valuable to the extent that one does not merely insist that factual inferences from one level to another are legitimate but seriously tries to meet the arguments which go to show that they are not. If this can be achieved, the only task that remains is to show, in each case, exactly how evidence and conclusion are related. At this point, the third of our methods develops into the fourth, the method of descriptive analysis. The difference between them is important so long as it remains an open question whether the procedures, which sustain our claim to knowledge, do or do not require a proof of their legitimacy. If it can be shown that they do not, in a way that satisfactorily disposes of the sceptic's alleged disproof, then it does not greatly matter whether we regard the need for analysis as superseding the demand for justification, or whether we make the justification consist in the analysis. Assuming this to be the result, the analytic method profits by being the heir of all the rest. But it comes into its inheritance only when most of the difficult work is done. It is a weakness of some contemporary philosophers that they allow it to succeed too soon.

Having said so much in general about the questions which confront us, it is time that we developed the argument for particular cases. We shall begin with the problem of perception.

CHAPTER III

PERCEPTION

(i)

Are physical objects directly perceived?

THE problem of perception, as the sceptic poses it, is
that of justifying our belief in the existence of the
physical objects which it is commonly taken for granted
that we perceive. In this, as in other cases, it is maintained that there is a gap, of a logically perplexing kind,
between the evidence with which we start and the
conclusions that we reach. If the conclusions are
suspect, it is because of the way in which they seem
to go beyond the evidence on which they depend. The
starting-point of the argument is, as we have seen, that
our access to the objects whose existence is in question
must be indirect.

In the case of perception, however, it may well be
doubted whether this premise is acceptable. There
appears to be no harm in saying that our belief in the
existence of such things as chairs and tables is founded
on the evidence of our senses ; but if this talk of
evidence is meant to imply that such a belief is always
an inference from something else, it begs a disputed
question. And even allowing that this is a case in which
one can separate evidence and conclusion, it has yet to be
shown that there is a difference of level between them.
It is certainly not obvious that there is any question
here of a passage from one type of object to another.

Nevertheless, a great many philosophers have held

that this was so. From John Locke onwards, those who have sought to erect an edifice of knowledge on the basis of what Bertrand Russell, himself an exponent of this method, has called 'hard data', have commonly agreed that such data were yielded by sense-perception ; but they have also agreed that they did not include physical objects. Taking the hard data to be securely known, they have regarded the existence of physical objects as being relatively problematic.

This point may be obscured by the fact that philosophers of this way of thinking have allowed themselves to refer to their hard data by the use of words which are normally taken to stand for physical objects. Thus Berkeley claimed to follow common sense in holding that such things as trees and stones and houses were directly perceived. But if we consider what is ordinarily meant by a physical object of this kind, I think that we must admit that the class comprises only such things as are accessible, at least in theory, to more than one sense and to more than one observer. Various other properties are requisite, including that of occupying space and of having more than a momentary duration, but for the purpose of our argument it is the feature of publicity that is the most important. If anything perceptible is properly to be called a physical object, it must at least make sense to say of it that it is perceived by different people and that it is, for example, touched as well as seen. But these conditions are not satisfied by the objects which Berkeley, and most other philosophers, have regarded as hard data. What, according to them, is immediately given in perception is an evanescent object called an idea, or an impression, or a presentation, or a sense-datum, which is not only private to a single observer but private to a single sense.

This contention that we directly perceive sense-data, rather than physical objects, is not easy to interpret. The first thing to be noted is that, whether true or false, it is not an empirical statement of fact. A philosopher who thinks that he directly perceives physical objects does not for that reason expect anything different to happen from what is expected by one who believes that he directly perceives sense-data. Each is claiming to give an account of all perceptual experience, whatever form it may take, so that no experiment can settle the issue between them. Neither can the statement that only sense-data are directly perceived be interpreted as a reflection on the ordinary usage of sensory verbs like 'hear' and 'touch' and 'see'. Or rather, if it were so interpreted, it would be obviously false. It is true that there is a familiar use of words like 'hear' and 'taste' and 'smell', according to which the objects that are heard or tasted or smelled are private to a single sense. We commonly talk of hearing sounds, as well as of hearing the things that make the sounds, and whereas the things that make the sounds can be perceived in other ways besides, the sounds themselves can only be heard. But neither sounds nor tastes nor smells are ordinarily regarded as being private to a single observer; it makes perfectly good sense to speak of two different persons hearing the same sound or smelling the same smell. The only sounds that are by nature private to a single observer are those that he hears in his mind's ear, those, in fact, that make no sound at all. And when we come to the most important senses, those of sight and touch, we find that ordinary usage does not provide them with accusatives on the analogy of sound and hearing. One may speak indifferently of hearing a clock or of hearing its tick, but one does not speak of touching the feel of a clock or of seeing its look. What one is ordinarily said to touch and see is the clock itself. And the clock which is seen is the very same object as the clock which is touched. There are objects such as mirror-images which are private to the sense of sight, but they again are not private to a single observer. It is only the things that one sees in one's mind's eye that are exclusively one's own.

Thus it appears that those who would have us say that the only immediate objects of perception are sense-data are making a considerable departure from ordinary usage. They are assimilating all forms of perception to the possession of mental images ; thereby achieving the paradoxical result of taking as the standard case of sense-perception something that is ordinarily con-trasted with it. We can say, if we like, that they are making a linguistic recommendation. By giving them new accusatives they are introducing a special usage of sensory words like 'hear' and 'touch' and 'see'. But this is not for them a mere matter of caprice. If they make the recommendation, it is because they feel bound to make it ; they feel that the introduction of these accusatives is somehow forced upon them by the facts, that it alone permits them to give an adequate account of what perception is. The question is why it should be thought that this is so.

(ii)

The argument from illusion

If we examine the reasons which philosophers have in fact given in favour of the view that only sense-data are directly perceived, we find that they mainly rest upon what is known as the argument from illusion. The starting-point of this argument is that objects appear differently to different observers, or differently to the same observer under different conditions, and further, that the way in which they appear is causally dependent upon extraneous factors such as the presence of light, the position of the observer, or the state of his nervous system. These premises themselves are not likely to be questioned. The difficulty is to see how they can lead to the desired result.

Now considering first the fact that appearances vary, we may argue that this proves at least that people sometimes do not perceive things as they really are. If, to take a familiar example, a coin looks at the same time round to one person and, from a different angle, elliptical to another, it follows that it is to one of them at least presenting a deceptive appearance. The coin may in fact be neither round nor elliptical; it cannot in any case be both. So that if each of these persons judges that he is perceiving the coin as it really is, at least one of them will be undergoing an illusion. It is not, however, necessary to the argument that anyone should ever actually be deceived by an experience of this kind. It is not necessary to it even that the appearance of a physical object should ever actually vary. All that is required is that it be possible that it should. It is enough that it makes sense to say of the coin that it looks at the same time round to one person and elliptical to another, whether or not this ever occurs in fact. Perhaps if such things never did occur, we should not have this usage; but that is irrelevant. The point is that we do have it, and that thereby we admit the possibility that physical objects may appear to people otherwise than as they really are.

But to say that an object may sometimes appear to be what it is not does not imply that we never perceive it as it really is, still less that what we directly perceive is never the object itself but something else. To obtain this last result one has to make the ruling that in every case in which an object seems to be perceived there is something which is directly perceived, and also that what is directly perceived cannot appear otherwise than as it is. One will then be able to conclude that whenever a physical object appears differently from what it is, something other than it is being directly perceived. Even so, it will not follow that a physical object cannot ever be directly perceived; for there is nothing in the argument, so far developed, to show that we never do, or can, perceive the object as it really is: all that has been established is that we sometimes may not. At this point, however, we are invited to take notice of the similarity which obtains between the cases, if there are any, in which the object appears in its true guise and those in which it does not. From different angles the coin may appear a variety of different shapes: let it be assumed that one of them is the shape that it really is. There will be nothing to mark off this appearance from the others except a difference of aspect which may be extremely slight. There will in any case be no such difference between the way in which the coin is perceived in this instance and the way in which it is perceived in all the others as to render it at all plausible to say that they are generically distinct; that the object which is directly perceived in this instance is of a different kind altogether from that which is directly perceived in all the others. But, since only one of the appearances can fail to be deceptive, we must allow that in all but one of the instances it is not the physical

object itself that is directly perceived. And if we are
willing to admit that the instances are all sufficiently
alike for it to be reasonable to hold that an object of
the same type is directly perceived in every case, it will
follow that the physical object is not directly perceived in the remaining instance either. In this way
we are brought to the conclusion that, even granting
that physical objects may sometimes be perceived as
they really are, what is directly perceived is always
something else.

This argument is plainly not conclusive, but I think
that it has much persuasive force, provided always that
we accept the ruling that when a physical object appears
in any way other than it is, it is not itself directly perceived. But why should we accept this ruling? It
makes perfectly good sense to talk of perceiving things
which look in some way different from what they are,
and there is at least no obvious reason why we should
here feel bound to add that these things are not perceived directly. It is not clear even what 'direct
perception' is supposed to mean, if I do not directly
perceive the things at which I am directly looking,
however deceptive their appearances may be. The
suggestion seems to be that the object interposes its
appearance, like a sheet of glass, between itself and the
observer. The glass may be so frosted that we are
left in doubt as to the character, or even the existence,
of what lies behind it : or it may be so transparent that
we hardly realize that it is there at all. We are to
think of physical objects as detachable from their
looks, or from their tactual qualities, in the way that
they are detachable from the sounds that they may
make. Even this, as we have seen, does not bring in
sense-data, but it takes a large step towards them. It

is, I think, a move that can be made; but if all we
had to go upon were the fact that physical objects may
appear otherwise than as they are, there would seem
to be little reason for our making it.

A further motive is provided by the possibility of
complete hallucinations. The case which we have so
far been considering is that in which a physical object
looks to have some quality that it does not really
have: there has been no question of its not being
really there to be perceived. But it may also happen
that one 'perceives' a physical object which is not
there at all. Let us take as an example Macbeth's
visionary dagger: since we are concerned only with
what is possible, the fact that this episode may be
fictitious does not matter. There is an obvious sense
in which Macbeth did not see a dagger; he did not
see a dagger for the sufficient reason that there was no
dagger there for him to see. There is another sense,
however, in which it may quite properly be said that
he did see a dagger; to say that he saw a dagger is
quite a natural way of describing his experience. But
still not a real dagger; not a physical object; not even
the look of a physical object, if looks are open to all
to see. If we are to say that he saw anything, it must
have been something that was accessible to him alone,
something that existed only so long as this particular
experience lasted; in short, a sense-datum. But then,
it is argued, there would not have been anything in the
character of the experience, considered simply in itself,
to differentiate it from one that was not delusive. It is
because an experience of this sort is like the experience
of seeing a real physical object that hallucinations are
possible. But in so far as the experiences are alike,
their analysis should follow the same pattern. So if we

are bound in one case to say that what is seen is a sense-datum, it is reasonable to hold that this is so in all.

But the fact is that in giving an account of such hallucinations we are not bound to say that anything is seen. It would be perfectly legitimate to describe Macbeth's experience by saying that he thought he was seeing a dagger, whereas in fact he was not seeing anything. It is just as natural a way of putting it as the other. And even if we insist on saying that he was seeing something, though not of course a physical object, we are not bound to infer from this that there *was* something which he saw; any more than we are bound to infer that ghosts exist from the fact that people see them. In general, we do use words like 'see' in such a way that from the fact that something is seen it follows that it exists. For this reason, if one does not believe in ghosts, one will be more inclined, in reporting a ghost story, to say that the victim thought he saw a ghost than that he did see one. But the other usage is not incorrect. One can describe someone as having seen a ghost without being committed to asserting that there was a ghost which he saw. And the same applies to Macbeth's visionary dagger or to any other example of this sort. It is only if we artificially combine the decision to say that the victim of a hallucination is seeing something with the ruling that what is seen must exist, that we secure the introduction of sense-data. But once again there seems to be no good reason why we should do this.

The position may be thought to change, however, when one brings in the causal aspect of the argument from illusion. For this is taken to prove that we never come near to perceiving a physical object as it really is, or at least that we have no reason to suppose that

we ever do. And if this were so, our inclination to say
that what we perceive does often have the properties
that it appears to have might lead us to conclude that
physical objects themselves were not perceived. But
this would conflict with our very strong inclination
to say that they are. An attempt, therefore, may be
made to resolve the difficulty by saying that physical
objects are indeed perceived, but only indirectly. What
is directly perceived, being dependent for its existence
on the state of the observer's nervous system, may
then be held to be a sense-datum.

This causal argument has been charged with in-
consistency on the ground that the physiological facts,
which it relies on, are facts about physical objects ;
and our knowledge of these facts is gained through
perception. But the question is not, at this stage,
whether we know anything about the character of
physical objects but *how* we know it ; and to say that
we know it through perceiving them does not commit
us to saying that this perception of them is direct. It
is true that the assumption that it is indirect raises
problems of its own, which we shall consider when we
come to deal with the causal theory of perception ; and
it is true also that the scientific information, on which
the causal argument draws, has its source in the naïve
realism of common sense. But even if it could be
shown that these scientific theories were not merely
historically but logically based upon naïve realism, this
would not protect it from them. On the contrary, as
Russell has succinctly put it : 'Naïve realism leads to
physics, and physics, if true, shows that naïve realism is
false. Therefore naïve realism, if true, is false ; therefore it is false.' [1]

[1] Bertrand Russell, *An Inquiry into Meaning and Truth*, p. 15.

But is it the case that 'physics, if true, shows that
naïve realism is false'? What physics shows, if it is
true, is that the way in which things appear to us is
causally conditioned by a number of factors which are
extraneous to the thing itself. If, for example, this
carpet now looks blue to me it is because light of a
certain wave-length is being transmitted from it to my
eyes, from which impulses pass along the appropriate
nerve fibres to my brain. In a different light, or if my
eyes or brain were injured, it might appear to me a
different colour, or no identifiable colour at all. But
to infer from this that we do not perceive things as they
really are, that, for example, the physical object which
I refer to as 'this carpet' is not really blue, is to make
the assumption that if a thing's appearing to have a
certain property is caused, in part, by outside factors,
then it does not really have it. Stated generally, this
assumption is obviously false. Thus, part of the cause
of the carpet's now appearing blue to me may be that
it has been dyed : but no one would regard this causal
dependence on the performance of the dyeing machine
as a reason for concluding that the carpet was not
really blue. It may be thought, however, that the
assumption does hold in the special case where the outside factors are to be found in the condition of the
observer. The idea at work is that if the object owes
its properties to us, they are not legally its own. But
what it owes, or partly owes, to the observer is its
appearing to him in the way it does : and if, to revert
to our example, this does not lead us to deny that the
carpet really *looks* blue, it is not clear why it should
lead us to deny that the carpet really *is* blue. There
are criteria for deciding what colour things 'really'
are ; it is mainly a question of the colour they appear

to be under what are regarded as normal conditions. The fact that the causal explanation of these appearances brings in the observer does not prevent these criteria from being satisfied; neither, therefore, does it prevent things from really having the colours that we ascribe to them. And the same would apply to any of the other properties with which things are credited by common sense. It would seem, therefore, that physics does not refute naïve realism, in the sense that it shows it to be false. Physics does not prove that we do not perceive physical objects as they really are. We shall see presently, however, that it does undermine naïve realism by casting doubt upon the adequacy of the picture which the naïve realist forms of the external world. The tendency is then to substitute the picture which is associated with the causal theory of perception : but this, as we shall also see, is hardly an improvement.

A variant of the causal argument, which has impressed some philosophers, adduces the fact that light takes time to travel. From this it is inferred that we do not see physical objects as they really are at the time at which we see them, but only, at best, as they were some time before. In the case of objects which are close at hand this difference in time is negligibly small, so small that it is doubtful if it warrants the conclusion that we do not see these objects in the state in which they are, but there are other cases in which it is appreciable. An instance which Russell often cites is that of the sun which we see only as it was eight minutes before : when it comes to remote stars the difference may amount to thousands of years. It may even happen that by the time we see it the star has ceased to exist. But if the star no longer exists, we

cannot, so it is argued, now be seeing it; and since in
every case in which the light has had an appreciable
distance to travel it is possible that the object which
we think that we are seeing has gone out of existence
in the interval, we cannot ever identify it with what
we see: for our present experience will be the same,
whether the object still exists or not. But if, in these
cases, we are not to say that we see the physical object,
then we should not say it even in the cases where the
time interval is negligibly small; for the comparative
length of the interval makes no difference to the character of our experience: there would be no justification for maintaining that we saw an object of one kind
when the interval was very short, and an object of an
entirely different kind when it was somewhat longer.
At what point in the continuous series of possible time
intervals would this fundamental change take place?
Once more, however, it seems too paradoxical to deny
that we see physical objects in any sense at all. So
again the solution offered is that we see them only indirectly: what we directly see is something else.

This argument draws its strength from the fact
that one tends to think of seeing as concerned only with
the present. It is assumed that, unlike our memories
or our imaginations, our eyes cannot range into the
past: whatever it is that we see must exist here and
now if it exists at all. But this assumption is not unassailable. Why should it not be admitted that our eyes
can range into the past, if all that is meant by this is
that the time at which we see things may be later than
the time when they are in the states in which we see
them? And having admitted this, why then should we
not also admit that it is possible to see things which
no longer exist? Such ideas might never have occurred

H

to us were it not for the discoveries of physics ; but once these physical facts are recognized, it does not seem too hard to adapt our way of speaking to them. We have to balance the oddity of saying that we can see what is past against the oddity of saying that we do not see physical objects ; and to give our eyes access to the past may well seem the more reasonable course.

The result of this discussion is that the arguments so far put forward do not make it excessively uncomfortable to hold the position of naïve realism. It will, however, need a little sophistication. We must be prepared to say that we do not always perceive things as they are ; that sometimes we see them only as they were, and sometimes as they neither are nor were ; that what we see, or otherwise perceive, may not exist, or else that we may think that we are perceiving something when we are not in fact perceiving anything at all ; and that the physical objects which we do perceive may owe some of their properties in part to the conditions which attend our perception of them. Of these admissions the last is perhaps the most difficult to make ; but not so difficult that, even when combined with the others, it should drive us, without further argument, into putting up a screen of sense-data between ourselves and the physical world.

(iii)

A method of introducing sense-data

The argument from illusion may, however, be developed in a simpler, but also more effective, way. We have already remarked, in the course of discussing the ques-

tion whether any statements are incorrigible, that the
ordinary way of describing what one perceives appears
to make a stronger claim than the perception itself can
cover. This follows indeed from the fact that illusions
are possible. If I can be undergoing an illusion when,
on the basis of my present experience, I judge, for
example, that my cigarette case is lying on the table in
front of me, I may, in saying that I see the cigarette
case, be claiming more than the experience strictly
warrants : it is logically consistent with my having just
this experience that there should not really be a
cigarette case there, or indeed any physical object at
all. It may be suggested, therefore, that if I wish to
give a strict account of my present visual experience, I
must make a more cautious statement. I must say
not that I see the cigarette case, if this is to carry the
implication that there is a cigarette case there, but only
that it seems to me that I am seeing it. We are not
here concerned with the question whether such statements are incorrigible ; we have already found reason
to hold that they are not. Their point is not that they
give us complete security from error ; it is that, if they
are true, they serve as descriptions of the contents of
our sense-experiences, irrespective of any larger claims
that these experiences may normally induce us to make.

Because of the possibility of illusion, it will not
necessarily be true that whenever it seems to me that I
am perceiving something, I really am perceiving it.
On the other hand, the converse is intended to hold.
From the statement that I see the cigarette case it is
supposed to follow that it seems to me that I see it.
Or, if this cannot be maintained, it is at least supposed
to follow that it seems to me that I see something
or other. It is to be a necessary fact that whenever

anything is perceived something must, in this sense, seem to be perceived. But whether this entailment really holds is a question which we shall have presently to examine.

The next step, continuing with our example, is to convert the sentence 'it now seems to me that I see a cigarette case' into 'I am now seeing a seeming-cigarette case'. And this seeming-cigarette case, which lives only in my present experience, is an example of a sense-datum. Applying this procedure to all cases of perception, whether veridical or delusive, one obtains the result that whenever anyone perceives, or thinks that he perceives, a physical object, he must at least be, in the appropriate sense, perceiving a seeming-object. These seeming-objects are sense-data; and the conclusion may be more simply expressed by saying that it is always sense-data that are directly perceived.

If this conclusion is allowed to be legitimate, it still does not follow that naïve realism is false. The naïve realist can, indeed, be refuted if he is made, as by Professor Price,[1] to adopt the view that visual and tactual sense-data are parts of the surfaces of physical objects. All that is then needed is to point out that the properties which are, by definition, ascribed to the surfaces of physical objects are inconsistent with those that are ascribed to sense-data. For instance, the surface of a physical object can exist without being perceived, but this cannot be said of a sense-datum. Price forces this untenable position upon the naïve realist because he attributes to him the view that physical objects are directly perceived; and so, being himself persuaded that sense-data are directly perceived, he concludes that the naïve realist must be maintaining

[1] H. H. Price, *Perception*, ch. 2.

that sense-data and physical objects are somehow identical. But the naïve realist, if he is circumspect, will not distinguish in this way between direct and indirect perception. His thesis must be that our ordinary way of speaking, in which this distinction is not made, is perfectly adequate for describing all the facts; and we have indeed seen that this standpoint can be maintained. All the same, if the procedure which leads to the introduction of sense-data is legitimate, the naïve realist by refusing to follow it denies us an insight into the analysis of perceptual statements. His method of describing the facts, though adequate in one sense, is not so in another: for there are important distinctions which it fails to bring to light. It has, indeed, the advantage that it shields us from a difficult problem; there is no question for the naïve realist of anything's ever seeming to come between us and the physical world. But philosophical problems are not settled simply by our taking care that they should not arise. If the introduction of sense-data is permissible, then there exists a problem about the way in which they are related to physical objects. If this question can be raised, it is philosophically entitled to an answer.

But can it be raised? The steps which are supposed to lead us to talk about sense-data are each of them open to challenge. Consider first the claim that in making such a statement as that I see my cigarette case, I assert more than is strictly warranted by the content of my present experience. This may well provoke the objection that it is not at all obvious what we are to understand by such an expression as 'the content of my present experience'. If I am asked what experiences I am having at this moment, and if I

interpret this somewhat unusual question as requiring
me to say, among other things, what it is that I see, I
shall answer quite correctly if I say that, among other
things, I see a cigarette case. But if this answer is
correct, then, in saying that I see a cigarette case, I am
not doing more than describe my present experience.
Yet it does seem that there is a sense in which I could
be having just this experience, even though I was not
seeing any physical object at all. But if this is to
be said, we must give 'the content of experience' a
narrower interpretation. We must take it to refer, in
this instance, only to what is 'visually given' to me,
irrespective of its connection with anything else. The
question is whether such an interpretation is intelligible.

Many philosophers would say that it was not.
Professor Ryle, for example, argues that 'the verb "to
see" does not signify an experience, *i.e.* something
that I go through, am engaged in. It does not signify
a sub-stretch of my life-story.' [1]   In the same spirit he
maintains that 'neither the physiologist nor the psychologist nor I myself can catch me in the act of seeing
a tree — for seeing a tree is not the sort of thing in
which I can be caught'. Seeing something is not 'an
introspective phenomenon' nor is it 'an eccentric sort
of state or process'. It is not a phenomenon, or a
state, or a process of any kind at all.[2] Consequently,
anyone who tries to pin-point an experience of seeing
is making a logical mistake. He is trying to delimit
something which could not exist.

Professor Ryle's reason for saying this is that the
verb 'to see', like other verbs of 'perceptual detection',
is used to signify not that anything is going on but

[1] G. Ryle, *Dilemmas*, p. 103.
[2] *Ibid.* p. 102.

rather that something has been accomplished. He quotes with approval Aristotle's remark that 'I can say "I have seen it" as soon as I can say "I see it"'. In the same way, to score a goal is to have scored it, to win a race is to have won it. And just as there is no state or process of winning a race, over and above the process of running it faster than the other competitors, so there is no process of seeing a thing apart from the process of looking at it. One can look at things without seeing them; one may be careless or inattentive or distracted. But this does not mean that one has failed to carry out some process in addition to the looking, any more than if one runs without winning one has failed to carry out some process in addition to the running. To look and see is not to look and do something else, subsequently or at the same time; it is to look successfully.

In support of this view Ryle points out that the words 'see' and 'hear' are not ordinarily used in the continuous present or past tenses. One says that one sees or hears something, not that one is seeing or hearing it. At least, not normally; as against Ryle, I should maintain that the use of the continuous tense was rare, rather than incorrect. Neither does his point apply to the other verbs of perceptual detection: there is nothing even unusual about saying that one is touching, or tasting, or smelling, or feeling whatever it may be. Ryle's answer to this might be that verbs like 'touch' and 'taste' do double duty. They have a use corresponding to that of 'look' in which they designate a state or process, and a use corresponding to that of 'see' in which they designate an achievement; and he may maintain that it is only when they are used in the first of these ways that they can be put into the continuous tense. He, however, is concerned only with the use in which they designate achievements, and the error which he attributes to most other philosophers is that of mistaking these achievements for experiences.

But even granting that verbs of perceptual detection are most commonly used in the way that Ryle suggests, it still does not follow that the experiences which philosophers have supposed that they describe do not exist. The most that follows is that these experiences have been misdescribed. We must not talk of the experience of seeing something, for it is a misuse of the verb 'to see' to make it stand for a state or process. Very well; let us find some other words. Let us talk of the experience of 'having something in sight', and let us make this artificial expression do the work for which philosophers have improperly enlisted the verb 'to see'. At the present moment, for example, I am looking at a piece of paper; I see it, and so long as I succeed in seeing it, I am having it in sight. Whatever may be said of the ordinary use of the verb 'to see', 'to have something in sight', in the sense which I am giving to this expression, does signify 'something that I go through, am engaged in', in short, an experience. Of course it is one thing to invent an expression and another to prove that it has application. It may still be argued that there could be no such experience as I am trying to describe. To which I can only answer that there is such an experience since I am at this moment undergoing it. It is an experience of a type which is perfectly familiar to anyone who can see; and the fact, if it be a fact, that our ordinary talk of seeing does not describe it is not a justification for conjuring it out of existence.

But even this does not give us quite what we want. For to say that I now have a piece of paper in sight seems to imply that there is a piece of paper there.

Whereas the experience which I am trying to find words for would be the same whether the piece of paper were really there or not. In the sense in which I now have this piece of paper in sight, it can equally well be said of Macbeth that he had his dagger in sight. If we are to speak for this purpose of having things in sight, the expression must be understood in such a way that the existence of the physical object which appears to be referred to remains an open question: there is no implication either that it does exist or that it does not. And the same applies to the other senses. If I am not allowed to say that I am now having the experience of hearing the sound of a human voice, on the ground that the verb 'to hear' is not ordinarily used to signify an experience, I must have recourse to some such artificial expression as that I have the sound of a human voice in hearing. But again, if it is to serve to delimit my experience, this expression must be understood in such a way that it remains an open question whether any human voice is really making the sound, or indeed whether there is any sound at all, in the usual sense in which for there to be a sound it must be open for all to hear. It must not be implied either that such a sound really is being made or that it is not; only that I now have it in hearing.

Neither is it implied that I make any judgement about the character of the experience. Apart from any difficulties that may be raised about the use of verbs of perceptual detection, the drawback to employing such a formula as 'it seems to me that I now see a cigarette case' for the description of one's experience is that the phrase 'it seems to me' most often serves to express a tentative opinion. One uses it in the cases where one is hesitant about the identification of what one is perceiving. It would be considered odd for me to say 'it seems to me that I now see a cigarette case' if I had in fact no doubt that I did see one. But the oddity is not so great that there need be excessive difficulty in understanding what is meant. We are to use the expression 'it seems that' as a means of signifying how things look, or feel, or otherwise appear, irrespective of any judgement that one may be led to make about their physical existence, or of the degree of confidence with which one makes it. And here to say that a thing appears to be such and such is not equivalent to saying that one is inclined to judge that it really is such and such. No doubt we do have a general tendency to judge that things are as they appear to be; it can be argued even that it is a universal tendency, with the proviso that it is inhibited in the relatively infrequent cases where the conditions are known to be abnormal. But this does not mean that this tendency *constitutes* the way that things appear. In the sense in which the word 'appear' is here being used, the way that things appear supplies both the cause of our tendency to judge that they really are whatever it may be and the ground for the validity of these judgements. The judgements are not to be identified with their grounds, nor the tendency with its cause. The mistake of so identifying them may be accounted for by the fact that the word 'appear' is frequently, perhaps most frequently, used in a different sense, the sense in which the dictionary defines it as 'to be in one's opinion': for our purposes, therefore, it has the same drawback as the verb 'to seem'. Not that the sense in which we are using it is entirely unfamiliar; and if it were, it would not matter to the argument.

Though we judge how things are on the basis of

their appearances, we do not invariably judge that they
are what they appear to be. Even if we have a natural
inclination always so to judge, it is an inclination that
is sometimes checked. We admit the possibility that
a thing which we perceive may, for example, look unlike
itself. Not only may it appear to have some property
which it does not really have, but it may look like some
quite different thing. Sometimes we are deceived by
this, and sometimes not. In any event, it follows that
it need not always be true that when one sees something it also seems to one that one sees it. In the sense
which we are giving to the expression 'it seems that',
this will indeed be true in the normal cases where a
thing looks to be what it is : but it will not be true in
the cases where it looks to be a different thing. Nevertheless even in these cases there will be something that
it looks to be. It is not possible that one should see a
physical object without its displaying a look of some
kind, any more than one can hear it without its
ostensibly making any sound. From the fact that I
now have a given thing in sight it does, therefore,
follow that it now seems to me that I have something in
sight, even though this 'something' may not be the
same as the thing in question. And this applies also
to the other forms of sense-perception. If I perceive a
physical object in any way it will follow that it seems
to me that I perceive something in that way, though
not necessarily the same thing as I do perceive.

To this it may be objected that we very often discover, through perception, how physical objects are,
without thereby discovering how they seem.[1] Glancing

---

[1] Cf. R. A. Wollheim, 'The Difference between Sensing and
Observing', *Supplementary Proceedings of the Aristotelian Society*, vol.
xxviii.

at the table in front of me, I now see a number of
objects which I have no difficulty in identifying. I can
say what properties they have, that, for example, this
ink-pot is half-full, or that the book beside it has a
yellow jacket. But if I am asked how these things now
look to me, I may well be at a loss for an answer. It
takes skill to observe the looks of things, as opposed to
the things themselves. Painters and some psychologists
acquire it ; they call our attention to appearances, and
bring to light details, which may otherwise escape our
notice. But the fact that these details can escape our
notice proves, surely, that to perceive a physical object
is not necessarily to perceive how it appears. It may
happen that when I perceive something it also seems
to me that I perceive either that or some other thing :
but one does not follow from the other. It is possible
for me to perceive a physical object without its seeming
to me to be like anything at all.

I do not think that this objection holds. Certainly
there is a sense in which one may notice things without
noticing their appearance. One can describe what one
sees, without perhaps being able to say exactly how it
looks. But from the fact that I am not trained to make
accurate judgements about the way things look, it does
not follow that I can see them without their displaying
any look to me at all. To say that it seems to me that I
see something is, in the present context, to say no more
than that I have something in sight, in a sense of having
something in sight which leaves it open whether what
I have in sight really is the physical object that I may
take it to be. It is surely not possible to see anything
without, in this sense, having it in sight. And this
means that it is not possible for anyone to see a physical
object, without its seeming to him that he sees it.

The fact that he may not notice how it looks to him is irrelevant. To take an analogy, if I am interested in a book that I am reading I may not notice how it is printed ; but it does not follow that I can read the book without having the print in sight.

I conclude then that this step in the process of arriving at sense-data can be made good. In a suitable sense of 'seeming', it can be allowed that whenever anyone perceives, or thinks that he perceives, a physical object, it must then seem to him that he perceives something or other. It is not, however, necessarily true that whenever it seems to someone that he perceives something, he really does perceive a physical object ; for here we have to allow for the possibility of illusion. Thus, to say 'it seems to me that' is, in this context, to make a more cautious statement, not in the sense that one is expressing only a tentative opinion, but in the sense that one is making a smaller claim.

(iv)

Concerning the legitimacy of sense-data

What appears most dubious of all is the final step by which we are to pass from 'it seems to me that I perceive *x*' to 'I perceive a seeming-*x*', with the implication that there is a seeming-*x* which I perceive. Since the existence and character of these seeming things is not affected by the question whether the perception is veridical or delusive, or whether they are or are not perceived by any other person, or in any other conditions, or at any other time, they cannot be physical objects. They are momentary, private entities, created, it may well seem, only by a stroke of the pen,

yet threatening to imprison the observer within a circle
of his own consciousness. They may, therefore, fairly
be regarded as a nuisance, but this, as we have seen,
is not a justification for ignoring them. The question
which has now to be decided is whether their introduction is legitimate.

Again, many philosophers would say that it was not.
Professor Ryle once more may serve as an example.
His view about sense-data, with which, as we have
remarked, our seeming-things may be identified, is that
'this whole theory rests upon a logical howler, the
howler, namely, of assimilating the concept of sensation to the concept of observation'.[1] His reason for
thinking that this is a howler is that if observing something entails having a sensation, then having a sensation
cannot itself be a form of observation; for if it were, it
would in its turn entail having a further sensation and
we should be involved in an infinite regress. Moreover, the sort of thing that can be said about observation,
or perception, cannot significantly be said about sensation. 'When a person has been watching a horse-race,
it is proper to ask whether he had a good or a bad view
of it, whether he watched it carefully or carelessly and
whether he tried to see as much of it as he could.' But
no one asks questions of this sort about sensations,
'any more than any one asks how the first letter in
"London" is spelled'.[2] Sensations, although they can
be noticed and attended to, are not 'objects of observation', and 'having a sensation cannot itself be a species
of perceiving, finding or espying'.[3] This last statement is based on the assumption that it is impossible

[1] G. Ryle, *The Concept of Mind*, p. 213.
[2] *Ibid.* p. 207.
[3] *Ibid.* p. 214.

to perceive anything without having the appropriate
sensation, that to speak of someone's seeing something
without having any visual sensations, or of his hearing
something without having any auditory sensations,
would be self-contradictory. But Ryle himself subsequently decides that this assumption is false. His
reconsidered view is that the 'primary concept of sensation', the concept which we employ when, for example,
we speak of sensation returning to a numbed part of
the body, 'is not a component of the generic concept
of perception, since it is just a species of that genus'[1].
To have a sensation of this sort is just to feel something,
and since one can see and hear without feeling anything, seeing and hearing do not in this sense entail
having sensations. They may be accompanied by
sensations, such as a sense of strain in the eyes, or a
tingling in the ears, but these sensations are not representatives of what is seen or heard. Thus when philosophers speak, in the way they do, of visual and auditory
sensations, they must be using the word 'sensation' in
some more sophisticated sense. There might be no
harm in this if they still made the word apply to something, but that, according to Ryle, is just what they
fail to do. The 'impressions', to which they wish to
make it apply, do not exist. They are invented by
philosophers in the mistaken belief that something is
required to mediate between external objects and the
mind. 'Impressions are ghostly impulses, postulated
for the ends of a para-mechanical theory.'[2]

These arguments have commanded a fairly wide-
spread assent, but I do not myself think that they show
the introduction of sense-data to be illegitimate. In
the first place, it may be answered that even if it were

---

[1] *Ibid*. p. 242.   [2] *Ibid*. p. 243.

correct to say that the advocates of sense-data treat sensation as a form of observation, what must here be meant by observation is not something which itself entails sensation. It therefore does not follow that they are committed to an infinite regress. They have special reasons, as I have tried to show, for analysing the perception of physical objects into the 'sensing' of seeming-objects : but these reasons do not apply in turn to the sensing of seeming-objects. One is not obliged to analyse this into an awareness of seeming-seeming-objects ; there is no question of one's having to adopt the general rule that no object is approachable except through an intermediary. Ryle has indeed considered the possibility of some such defence ; and his rejoinder is that it 'in effect explains the having of sensations as the *not* having any sensations',[1] on the ground that if having a sensation is construed as an awareness of a sensible object, then one may have sensations without being sensitively affected. But this rejoinder seems to me very weak. For to talk of someone's sensing a sense-datum is intended to be another way of saying that he is sensitively affected ; the manner in which he is affected reappears as a property of the sense-datum : to demand that provision should also be made for his having a sensation is to require that the same thing should be said twice over.

But let us suppose that Ryle is right, and that sensing a sense-datum cannot be made to do duty for having a sensation. This will still not be a decisive objection to the sense-datum theory. For the theory does not in fact require that the two should be identified : it does not have to be interpreted as referring to sensa-

[1] *Op. cit.* p. 215.

tions at all. To talk of sense-data is to talk of the way things seem, in the special sense of 'seeming' that I have been trying to explain. And if it be granted that people can seem to perceive things, in this sense, the question whether this coincides with what is ordinarily meant by their having sensations may be treated as irrelevant. Neither is there any need for sense-datum theorists to hold that the sensing of sense data is a form of observation, if calling it a form of observation is to be taken to imply that everything that can significantly be said about seeing, hearing, and the rest, in the more familiar uses of these words, can also be said about it. Accordingly, Ryle's comments on the everyday vocabulary of sensation and perception need not trouble them. It is not as if they were trying to give an account of the ways in which this vocabulary is commonly made to work. They need not even be suggesting that it is in any way inadequate for the ordinary purposes of communication. Their own talk of sense-data, assuming it to be legitimate, is obviously far less practical. What they are doing is to redescribe the facts in a way that is supposed to bring to light distinctions, of philosophical interest, which the ordinary methods of description tend to conceal. In pursuing this course they may in some cases have been guilty of the confusions which Ryle attributes to them. But I do not think that he has succeeded in showing that these confusions are an essential ingredient in their theory.

The view that sense-data are mythical is sometimes upheld on psychological grounds. The experiments made by *gestalt* psychologists are adduced to show that Locke, who with his conception of 'simple ideas' may fairly be regarded as the principal ancestor of the sense-

I

datum theorists, was mistaken in supposing either that
the mind is actually supplied with unitary impressions
or that it is a merely passive receptor.[1] But the answer
to this is that the advocates of sense-data need not
commit themselves to any special psychological theory
about the character, or genesis, of what is sensibly
given. Their interest lies only in establishing that
there are seeming-objects, in the sense we have explained : it does not matter to them what particular
features these seeming-objects are empirically found to
have, or how they come to have them. Psychology
cannot be used to refute them : for their concept of
sense-data is intended to be so general that everything
that the psychologists may discover about the machinery
of perception is describable by its means.

Even so, there is something suspect about their
procedure. The transition from 'it now seems to me
that I see *x*' to 'there is a seeming-*x* which I now see'
may be defended on the ground that the second sentence
is merely a reformulation of the first, a reformulation
which it is convenient to make because it is simpler and
neater in the contexts for which such sentences might
be required to make nouns do the work of verbs, to
talk of sense-data rather than of how things seem to
people. But, if this is allowed, one must be careful to
say nothing about sense-data that cannot be translated
back into the terminology of seeming. The danger is
that these private objects, which have been brought
into existence as a matter of literary convenience,
become independent of their origin. Questions arise
about the criteria for the self-identity of these objects,
the means of distinguishing one of them from another,
the possibility of their changing, the duration of their

[1] *An Essay Concerning Human Understanding*, Book II.

existence ; and one may think that mere inspection of them will provide the answers. But the position is rather that until such questions have been answered there are no objects to inspect. It is from the way in which we *decide* to answer them that the term 'sense-datum' acquires a more definite use. But how are these decisions to be reached ? How, for example, are we to determine what is to count as one sense-datum ? At the present moment it seems to me that I see the walls of a house, covered with virginia creeper, and a rose tree climbing to an open window, and two dogs asleep upon a terrace, and a lawn bespeckled with buttercups and clover, and many other things besides ; and it seems to me that I hear, among other things, the buzzing of insects and the chirruping of birds. How many visual or auditory sense-data am I sensing ? And at what point are they replaced by others ? If one of the dogs seems to stir in its sleep does this create a new sense-datum for me or merely transform an old one ? And if it is to be new, do all the others remain the same ? Clearly the answers to these questions will be arbitrary ; the appearance of the whole frontage of the house may be treated as one sense-datum, or it may be divided into almost any number. The difficulty is to find a rule that would be generally applicable. It might be suggested, for example, that we should say that there were, for a given observer at any given moment, as many visual sense-data as there were features that he could visually discriminate : but this again raises the question of what is to count as a single feature. And similar objections may be made to any other ruling that I can think of. The correct reply may, therefore, be that these questions do not admit of a definite answer, any more than there is a definite

answer to the question how many parts a thing can
have, or how much it can change without altering its
identity. That is to say, there are no general rules
from which the answers to such questions can be
derived; but this does not mean that they cannot be
given answers in particular cases. In the present
instance, I can choose to speak of there being a sense-
datum of the rose tree, or a sense-datum of one of its
roses, or of one of the petals of the rose, or even just a
sense-datum of something red; the only condition is
that I in every case refer to something which it now
seems to me that I see. And if it be asked whether my
present contemplation of the rose tree yields me one
sense-datum of it, or a series, and if it is a series, how
many members it has, the answer once again is that
there can be as many as I choose to distinguish. No
single sense-datum can outlast the experience of which
it helps to make up the content; but then it is not
clear what is to count as one experience. I can distinguish the experience I am having now from those
that I have had at different times in the past, but if
I were asked how many experiences I had had, for
example, during the last five minutes, I should not
know what to answer: I should not know how to set
about counting. The question would appear to have
no meaning. It does not follow, however, that I cannot
at any given moment delimit some experience which
I am then having: the boundaries may be fluid, but
I can say confidently of certain things that they fall
within the experience, and of others that they do not.
And for our present purposes this may be all that is
required.

It must then be admitted that the notion of a sense-
datum is not precise. Moreover, it appears to borrow

what little precision it has from the way in which we talk about physical objects. If I can pick out my present sense-datum of a rose it is because roses are things for which there are established criteria of identity. It is, in fact, only by the use of expressions which refer to the perception of physical objects that we have given any meaning to talking of sense-data at all. And it is hard to see how else we could have proceeded if we were to have any hope of being intelligible. This seems to me, however, to be a matter of psychology rather than of logic. If one has to describe the use of an unfamiliar terminology, the description, in order to be informative, must be given in terms of what is already understood ; and we are all brought up to understand a form of language in which the perception of physical objects is treated as the standard case. But this is a contingent fact : it is surely not inconceivable that there should be a language in which sense-experiences were described by the use of purely qualitative expressions which carried no reference to the appearances of physical objects. Such a language would not be very useful, but it could be adequate for the description of any given experience. Neither do I see any reason *a priori* why someone who had devised it as a means of recording his own experiences should not succeed in teaching it to others. But even if I am mistaken on this point, it would not follow, as has sometimes been suggested, that the so-called language of sense-data had no function to fulfil. If it derives its meaning only from the use of sentences which refer to the perception of physical objects, then it cannot, indeed, be made the vehicle of an argument which would seek to prove that sentences which purport to refer to physical objects are themselves devoid of meaning. But no such argument is here being considered : the fact that it is meaningful to talk of physical objects is not in question. What is in question is the truth of statements which imply that physical objects are perceived, or rather the strength of the reasons that we can have for believing that such statements are true. And even if all talk about sense-data derived its meaning from talk about the perception of physical objects, it would not follow that the truth of a statement which implied that some physical object was perceived was, in any given instance, a logical condition of the truth of a statement which was merely descriptive of some sense-datum. Logically, the sense-datum statement might be true even though any given claim to perceive a physical object were false.

This question of the admissibility of sense-data is, I think, still worth discussing both for its own sake and because of the important part which it has played in the history of modern philosophy. It is, however, to be remarked that they are not strictly needed for the formulation of the sceptic's problem. Even if one refuses to take the final step of transforming 'seeming to perceive an object' into '"perceiving" a seeming-object', and inferring from this that there is a seeming-object which is directly perceived, there will still be the gap between evidence and conclusion which the sceptic requires. It is the gap between things as they seem and things as they are ; and the problem consists in our having to justify our claims to know how physical objects are on the basis of knowing only how they seem. In another aspect, it is the problem of setting out the relationship between perceiving a physical object and seeming to perceive it, in the sense we have explained. A problem of this sort must arise once it is admitted that our ordinary judgements of perception claim more than is strictly contained in the experiences on which they are based. We have seen that this assumption can be challenged, but the tendency of our discussion has been to show that it should be upheld.

(v)

Naïve realism and the causal theory of perception

The effect of this is that we admit the first step in the sceptic's argument, and in so doing we part company with naïve realism. We part company with it, not in the sense that we disallow the naïve realist's pretension to know what he thinks he knows, but simply by recognizing a distinction which he refuses to consider. For, as we have seen, it is characteristic of his philosophical position that he denies, or overlooks, the existence of the gap between what things seem to be, in our special sense of seeming, and what they really are. His mistake, if it is one, is therefore just that he oversimplifies the situation; he denies the possibility of questions which can in fact be asked.

The natural heir to naïve realism is the causal theory of perception. It is to this theory that people most commonly turn when they have been convinced that there are grounds for holding that physical objects are not directly perceived. To some extent, we have already dealt with it in considering the causal form of the argument from illusion. Its starting-point is that science proves that the objects which we should ordinarily say that we perceived, the objects which constitute the coloured, noisy, redolent world of common sense are very much our own creation. From this it may be inferred either that these are not physical objects at all, or else, more commonly, that they are physical objects in disguise. On this view, though we perceive physical objects, we do not perceive them in their natural states: they never appear in public unmade-up. We cannot remove this make-up, since our very presence is responsible for its being there, but we can theoretically discount it. We can allow for the influence of the medium of observation, and of the character and situation of the observer. And we can then work out what the object must itself be like in order to have, in such conditions, the effects on us that it does. It then turns out to be just what science tells us that it is. The famous distinction which Locke drew between primary and secondary qualities [1] is not a distinction between those perceived qualities that are unaffected by the conditions of observation and those that are affected. Since all are affected, there is no such distinction, as Berkeley realized.[2] The primary qualities of the object, those that literally characterize it, are, on this view, just those properties with which science credits it.

We have already seen that one of the foundations of the causal theory is unsound. From the fact that the perceived qualities of physical objects are causally dependent upon the state of the percipient, it does not follow that the object does not really have them. Accepting what the physiologists tell us, we are still not committed to holding that we cannot perceive physical objects as they really are. This does not mean, however, that we may not also be entitled to postulate

[1] *Op. cit.* Book II, ch. 8.
[2] *The Principles of Human Knowledge*, sections ix–xv.

an unperceived world of 'external' objects as a means
of accounting for our perceptual experiences. The
main philosophical objection to any such procedure is
that we cannot be justified in holding that things of
two different classes are causally connected when the
members of one of these classes, being unobservable,
never have been, or could be, found in conjunction
with the members of the other. But the answer to this
is that 'finding' an object need not here be construed
as observing it. It may be enough that there is indirect
evidence for its existence. Whether this is so or not
will depend upon the use that is made of the expressions
which are understood to refer to it. If, as in the
present case, they enter into theories which actually
serve to explain and predict phenomena, the introduction of such an object must be held to be legitimate.
And if one allows it to be a sufficient condition for two
things to be causally connected that one should be
explicable in terms of the other, one may properly refer
to these 'external' objects, in other words, to the
scientist's atoms and electrons, as the causes of our
perceptions. For this will just be a way of saying that
the occurrence and character of our perceptions can be
explained, to some degree at least, in terms of a theory
in which these objects figure. There are, indeed,
serious problems about the interpretation of the statements which constitute such a theory. It has to be
decided whether they can be reduced to statements
which do describe what is observable. And if, as we
may well expect, it turns out that they cannot be so
reduced, one will need to consider whether the things
to which they ostensibly refer must be taken to be real,
or whether it is still open to us to treat them as convenient fictions. There is also the question how the

authors of these statements can be justified, on the
basis of their observations, in putting them forward.
The proof that they are somehow justified is that they
do succeed in verifying them : but, as we have already
noted, this proof, like others of its kind, requires to be
defended against the sceptic's attack.

Assuming this defence to be successfully under-
taken, the causal theory is vindicated to the extent that
we are permitted to think of our sense-experiences as
having the objects envisaged by scientists for their
external causes ; but it still fails as a theory of perception. It fails for the reason that however strong the
evidence for the existence of these scientific entities
may be, our belief in the existence of such physical
objects as stones and trees and chairs and tables does
not depend upon it. We could give up all of current
physical theory without being logically committed to
denying the existence of things of these familiar sorts.
There would be no contradiction in denying that any
given set of statements about atoms and electrons was
true, or even meaningful, while at the same time
maintaining the truth of statements which affirm the
existence of the physical objects which we claim to
perceive. And from this it follows that, whatever may
be said in defence of the causal theory, it cannot be
regarded as furnishing an analysis of our perceptual
judgements. It may provide an explanation of the
facts which make them true, but it tells us neither
what they mean nor how we are justified in accepting
them.

In its purely scientific aspect there need be no
conflict between the causal theory and naïve realism.
It is possible to maintain both that such things as
chairs and tables are directly perceived and that our

sense-experiences are causally dependent upon physical
processes which are not directly perceptible. This is,
indeed, a position which is very widely held, and it is
perfectly consistent. There is, however, a way in which
acceptance of the causal theory may work to the naïve
realist's disadvantage. It does so, as we have already
remarked, by spoiling the picture which he forms of the
external world. The naïve realist is not alone in thinking that the physical objects which he perceives continue
to exist when no one is perceiving them. His peculiarity
is that he pictures them as existing when they are not
perceived in exactly the same form as they normally
display when they are. This picture is not a logical
ingredient in his theory, but it is its natural accompaniment. The causal theorist casts doubts upon it by
suggesting that even though the object may still exist
when it has ceased to be perceived, it cannot reasonably
be thought of as retaining the properties which are
causally dependent on our perception of it. This
argument does not, indeed, demolish even the naïve
realist's picture. He can reply that since the object
does really have the properties which he perceives it
to have, whether he perceives it or not, he is only
picturing it as it is. But the reason why he can put
up this defence is that our criteria of reality are such
that, in this instance, we identify the properties which
the object really has with those that it appears to have
in what are taken to be normal conditions. By remov-
ing these conditions we do not change the character of
the object, but we may become uneasy about the
propriety of still depicting it in the form which it owes
to them. Again, the naïve realist may reply that he
is picturing it just as it would appear if he did perceive
it. But this is clearly a more sophisticated attitude.

It takes him, as we shall see, a step in the direction of phenomenalism.

The causal theory also has its accompanying picture. Following the suggestion that the physical objects which we are commonly supposed to perceive are somehow disguised by our perception of them, it represents their continued existence, when they are not being perceived, as a matter simply of their dropping their disguise. But this picture is muddled, in a way that the naïve realist's is not. It divests the object of its colour and its other secondary qualities, leaving a skeleton to occupy its spatial position. But if the perceptible colour of the object is to be taken from it, just because it is perceptible, so must its perceptible figure and extension. And if all its perceptible qualities are taken from it, while, for the same reason, all the objects in its neighbourhood are also bereft of theirs, its perceptible location vanishes too. There can be no half-measures in this case. If a curtain is to be drawn between things as they really are and things as we perceive them, if what we perceive is just the effects of these things on us, then the objects to which we have access in perception fall entirely on our side of the curtain and so does the space in which they are located. What remains on the other side is the world of scientific objects with its appropriate space. These worlds do not interpenetrate, though one may be regarded as accounting for the other. There is no reason why a model of the 'external' world should not include features which are drawn from the world that we perceive ; indeed, to the extent that the model is pictorial, this cannot be avoided. But confusion results when a composite picture is made out of the two of them. It is very misleading to suggest that physical objects appear before us disguised as their own effects. In fact, the metaphor of disguise is out of place in this instance. Once more, the acceptance of this metaphor is not an integral part of the causal theory, but it is habitually associated with it. Otherwise the causal theory is hardly a theory of perception at all, in the philosophical sense. It simply gives us the assurance that phenomena can be scientifically explained. The problems which it raises belong to the philosophy of science.

(vi)
Phenomenalism

In the sense in which it is compatible with naïve realism, the causal theory is compatible also with phenomenalism ; that is, with the thesis that physical objects are logical constructions out of sense-data, or, in other words, that the sceptic's gap is to be bridged by a reduction of the way things are to the way they seem. The phenomenalist need not deny that the manner in which sense-data occur can be explained in terms of entities which are not themselves observable ; he will, however, add that to talk about such unobservable entities is, in the end, to talk about sense-data. For the position which he takes is that every empirical statement about a physical object, whether it seems to refer to a scientific entity or to an object of the more familiar kind that we normally claim to perceive, is reducible to a statement, or set of statements, which refer exclusively to sense-data. And what he may be understood to mean by saying that a statement S is 'reducible' to a class of statements K is first that the members of K are on a lower epistemological level than

S, that is, that they refer to 'harder' data, and secondly that S and K are logically equivalent. The notion of logical equivalence is, in this context, not so clear as one could wish, but it requires at least that it should not be possible to find, or even to describe, a set of circumstances in which one of the statements in question would be true and its supposed equivalent false.

The first difficulty which the phenomenalist has to meet is that physical objects, unlike sense-data, can exist without being perceived. To say this is not to beg the question against Berkeley. It is simply that we so define our terms that unless a thing has the ability to exist unperceived it is not counted as a physical object. This is not in itself to say that anything satisfies this condition, and one might interpret Berkeley as maintaining that nothing except minds did satisfy it; that there were in fact no physical objects, or rather, that there could not be.[1] I doubt, however, if this interpretation would be altogether just to him. He did allow that things that commonly pass for physical objects could continue to exist when only God perceived them : and to say of something that it is perceived only by God is to say that it is not, in any ordinary sense, perceived at all. But, whatever Berkeley's position may have been, the phenomenalist does not deny that there are physical objects. His contention is just that, if there are any, they are constituted by sense-data. Whether there are any is a matter of empirical fact, which as such does not concern him. It is enough for him that there could be physical objects ; his problem is then to analyse the statements which refer to them. And here the fact that it is possible

[1] *The Principles of Human Knowledge* and *Three Dialogues between Hylas and Philonous*.

for physical objects to exist when they are not perceived introduces a complication into his analysis. It obliges him to hold that the statements about sense-data, into which, according to his programme, statements about physical objects are to be translated, are themselves predominantly hypothetical. They will for the most part have to state not that any sense-data are actually occurring, but only that in a given set of circumstances certain sense-data would occur. In other words, the majority of the statements will not describe how things actually do seem to anyone, but only how they would seem if the appropriate conditions were fulfilled.

Among hypothetical statements there are some that can be construed as statements of what is called material implication : this means that the statement is held to be true in every case except that in which the antecedent clause is true and the consequent false. But this will not do for the hypotheticals which the phenomenalist needs for his analysis. For it follows from the definition of material implication that a hypothetical of this sort is true if its antecedent is false ; so that if the phenomenalist's hypotheticals were of this sort, his theory would yield the absurd result that in the absence of an observer any statement whatsoever about a physical object would be true. The hypotheticals which he needs are subjunctive conditionals ; but their analysis presents a problem which has not yet been solved. This does not mean that he is not entitled to use them ; but the failure to provide a satisfactory analysis of them may be considered a weakness in his position.

Some critics base their objection to phenomenalism not so much on the difficulty of interpreting these subjunctive conditionals, as on the fact that they are brought in at all. They maintain that when statements

about physical objects are categorical, as they very
frequently are, no rendering of them, however complicated and ingenious, into merely hypothetical statements about sense-data can possibly be adequate. A
good example of this line of argument is to be found in
a paper by Mr. Isaiah Berlin.[1] 'Such a categorical
existential material object sentence', says Mr. Berlin,
'as, "The table is next door", or "There is a table
next door", is used at the very least to describe something which is occurring or being characterised at the
time of speaking . . .; and being characterised or
occurring, unless the contrary is specifically stated or
implied, not intermittently but continuously, and in
any case not "hypothetically". For to say that something is occurring hypothetically is a very artificial and
misleading way of saying that it is not, in the ordinary
sense, occurring at all. . . .'[2]

I confess that I cannot see that there is any logical
force in this objection. It is quite true that sentences
which express hypothetical statements about sense-data
are not being used to assert that any sense-data are
occurring, but it does not follow that they are not being
used to assert that any physical events are occurring,
or that any physical objects exist. On the contrary,
this is just what they do serve to assert, if phenomenalism is correct. There is no more difficulty
of principle in replacing categorical statements about
chairs and tables by hypothetical statements about
sense-data than there is in replacing categorical statements about electrons by hypothetical statements about
the results of physical experiments, or in replacing

[1] I. Berlin, 'Empirical Propositions and Hypothetical Statements',
Mind, vol. lix, no. 235.
[2] *Ibid.* pp. 300-301.

categorical statements about people's unconscious feelings by hypothetical statements about their overt
behaviour. Whether the translation can even theoretically be carried out in any of these instances is
another question. As we shall see, there are strong
reasons for concluding that the phenomenalist's 'reduction' is not feasible; but its possibility cannot
be excluded merely on the ground that it substitutes
hypothetical statements at one level for categorical
statements at another.

A puzzling feature of Mr. Berlin's own position is
that he is willing to allow, at least for the sake of argument, that categorical statements about physical objects
and hypothetical statements about sense-data may
'strictly entail' each other, which is surely all that any
phenomenalist requires. He objects only that even
if they do entail each other, they are not identical
in meaning, and in some legitimate sense of 'being
identical in meaning' he is no doubt right. His main
point is, I think, that statements of these different
types have, as it were, a different 'feel'. As he truly
says, 'common sense and the philosophers who are in
sympathy with it, have always felt dissatisfied [with
phenomenalism]. The reduction of material object
sentences into what we may, for short, call sense-datum
sentences, seemed to leave something out, to substitute
something intermittent and attenuated for something
solid and continuous.'[1] In fact, if the phenomenalists
are right, nothing is left out: any statement which
implies that there are solid and continuous objects in
the world will reappear in the form of the appropriate
statements about sense-data. But even if nothing
really is left out, it is natural that something should

[1] *Ibid*. p. 291.

K

seem to be. For there is no picture which is associated with phenomenalism in the way that the picture of things continuing to exist in much the same form as we perceive them is associated with naïve realism, or the picture of things existing stripped of their disguise is associated with the causal theory. John Stuart Mill, who held a phenomenalist position, summarized it by describing physical objects as 'permanent possibilities of sensation'.[1] But a permanent possibility of sensation is not something that can very well be pictured. In Plato's myth, the shadows on the wall of the cave, which are all that the prisoners can see, are contrasted with substantial objects outside.[2] Phenomenalism seems to leave us with nothing but the shadows.

But while this may account for the psychological resistance with which phenomenalists so very often meet, it does not show that their thesis is false. However hard they may make it for us to construct an imaginative picture of the physical world, they may still be right in claiming that statements about physical objects are reducible to statements about sense-data, that to talk about the way things are comes down in the end to talking about the way they would seem. The character of their thesis is, in a broad sense, logical, and it must be submitted to a logical examination. Even so, I do not think that it succeeds.

Let us begin by remarking one of the more obvious difficulties. In the most common case, where it is not implied that a physical object is actually being perceived, to describe it is supposed to be wholly a matter of saying how it would appear, that is, what sense-data there would be if certain conditions were fulfilled.

---

[1] *An Examination of Sir William Hamilton's Philosophy*, ch. 11.
[2] *Republic*, Book VII.

Roughly speaking, the conditions are those which are required for the object, if it exists, to be perceptible. But how are these conditions to be specified ? It is not enough for the phenomenalist to make such vague assertions as that what he means by saying that there is a table in the next room is that if he were there he would perceive it. For his being there is a matter of a physical body's being in a certain spatial relationship to other physical objects, and, on the assumption that to talk about physical objects is always to talk about sense-data, this situation must itself be described in purely sensory terms. But it is not at all easy to see how this could be done. One may avoid a part of the difficulty simply by eliminating any reference to an observer. This does not imply that there could be sense-data without observers : it must be remembered that we have not so far succeeded in giving any meaning to speaking of sense-data except as a way of describing how things seem to people ; so that, in any talk of this kind, some reference to an observer remains implicit. But the point is that it need not be explicit. There is no need to bring in a description of any particular person. It would, indeed, be incorrect to do so except in the cases where a particular person is actually mentioned in the statement to be analysed. The hypothetical observer must be, as it were, outside the picture. Otherwise we should have to reckon with the possibility that his presence would somehow affect the situation ; and clearly this would falsify the analysis.

But even if one need not mention the observer, one has still to 'place' the situation in which the observations are supposed to be made. One has to describe the setting in which the occurrence of certain sense-data is to be taken as establishing the existence of the physical object in question; and this description must be purely sensory. But it would seem hardly possible to find a set of sensory descriptions which would sufficiently distinguish one place from another. And when it comes to times the difficulty is even more obvious. Suppose, for example, that the problem were to give a phenomenalist translation of such a statement as that Julius Caesar crossed the Rubicon in 49 B.C. How would one set about rendering '49 B.C.' in purely sensory terms? To this the phenomenalist may reply that we do in fact succeed in identifying places and times by making observations; we note features of the landscape, look at watches and calendars, and so forth; and these performances in the end consist in our sensing sense-data. It does not follow, however, that any description of these sense-data would be sufficient to identify the place or time uniquely; and so long as no such description is found the phenomenalist's reduction has not been carried out.[1]

I do not dwell upon this point because it is only a special case of a more general difficulty, which is, I think, fatal to phenomenalism. If the phenomenalist is right, the existence of a physical object of a certain sort must be a sufficient condition for the occurrence, in the appropriate circumstances, of certain sense-data; there must, in short, be a deductive step from descriptions of physical reality to descriptions of possible, if not actual, appearances. And conversely, the occurrence of the sense-data must be a sufficient con-

---

[1] For a more thorough discussion of these difficulties see my paper on 'Phenomenalism', *Proceedings of the Aristotelian Society*, 1947–8. Reprinted in my *Philosophical Essays*. See also H. H. Price's review of *Philosophical Essays* in *The Philosophical Quarterly*, vol. v, no. 20.

dition for the existence of the physical object; there must be a deductive step from descriptions of actual, or at any rate possible, appearances to descriptions of physical reality. The decisive objection to phenomenalism is that neither of these requirements can be satisfied.

The denial that statements which imply the existence of physical objects can be logically deduced from any finite set of statements about sense-data is often expressed in the form that no statement about a physical object can be conclusively verified. It is alleged that while the probability of there being an illusion can be diminished to a point where it becomes negligible, its possibility is never formally excluded. However far they may be extended, our sense-experiences can never put beyond question the truth of any statement implying the existence of a physical object; it remains consistent with them that the statement be false. But is this really so? Can there be any doubt at all of the present existence of the table at which I am seated, the pen with which I am writing, the hand which is holding the pen? Surely I know for certain that these physical objects exist? And if I do know this for certain, I know it on the basis of my sense-experiences. Admittedly, my present experiences, taken by themselves, are not sufficient for the purpose: the mere fact that I now seem to see and feel a pen in my right hand does not prove conclusively that either of these objects exists. But when my present experiences are taken in conjunction with all my past experiences, then, it may plausibly be held, the evidence is sufficient; I am entitled to regard the existence of these and many other physical objects which I can now perceive as conclusively established.

In support of this view it may be argued that even if the run of favourable evidence were, as is logically possible, to come to an end, even if this object which I now take to be a table were henceforward to seem to me to be something quite different, or even to vanish altogether never to reappear, I still should not conclude that it never had existed; I should not conclude that the long and varied series of experiences on which my belief in its existence had been based were merely the symptoms of an obstinate illusion. I should regard the sudden transformation or disappearance of the table as a curious physical phenomenon for which I should seek a physical explanation. Even if from this moment onwards my experiences were entirely phantasmagoric, manifesting none of the coherence that they would have if I were perceiving physical objects, I still should not infer that all my previous perceptions had been delusive. If I did not doubt my own sanity, I should infer only that the world had mysteriously changed. As a result of the disappearance of the physical evidence, the un-favourable testimony of others, assuming for the sake of argument that it was still in some way available to me, or the vagaries of my memory, I might indeed be brought to doubt whether I had ever really had the experiences which supported my belief in the existence of physical objects; but that is beside the point. The point is that given that there is no doubt that I have had these experiences, there can be no doubt either that at the relevant times the physical objects which they seemed to reveal to me really did exist.

This argument does, I think, show that there comes a stage at which the suggestion that certain physical objects may not exist ceases, in the light of one's experience, to be a serious hypothesis. That is to say, it is a hypothesis which, whatever the further evidence, no sensible person would adopt. But this does not mean that it is formally excluded, that anyone who did adopt it would be contradicting himself. At the present moment there is indeed no doubt, so far as I am concerned, that this table, this piece of paper, this pen, this hand, and many other physical objects exist. I know that they exist, and I know it on the basis of my sense-experiences. Even so, it does not follow that the assertion of their existence, or of the existence of any one of them, is logically entailed by any description of my sense-experiences. The fuller such a description is made, assuming all the evidence to be favourable, the more far-fetched becomes the hypothesis that the physical object in question does not in fact exist; the harder it is, in short, to explain the appearances away. But this is still not to say that the possibility of explaining them away is ever *logically* absent. At what precise point would the suggested explanation cease to be merely fanciful and become formally incompatible with the evidence ? For the phenomenalist to succeed, he must be able to produce a specimen set of statements, describing the occurrence in particular conditions of certain specified sense-data, from which it follows logically that a given physical object exists. And I do not see how this is to be achieved.

But if it is doubtful whether the occurrence of a given series of sense-data can ever be a sufficient condition for the existence of a physical object, it is, I think, even more doubtful whether the existence of the physical object can be a sufficient condition for the occurrence of the sense-data. Those who think that it may be sufficient are assuming that with respect to any physical object which is capable of being perceived, it is possible to specify a set of conditions such that if any observer satisfies them he must perceive it. This point of view is expressed in a rough way by Berkeley when he claims that to say, for example, that the earth moves is to say that 'if we were placed in such and such cir- cumstances, and such or such a position and distance, both from the earth and the sun, we should perceive the former to move'.[1] But, setting aside the difficulty, which we have already noticed, of describing the cir- cumstances in purely sensory terms, it might very well happen that when we were placed in them we did not perceive the earth to move at all, not because it was not moving, but because we were inattentive, or look- ing in the wrong direction, or our view was in some way obscured, or because we were suffering from some physiological or psychological disorder. It might indeed be thought that such obstacles could be pro- vided for. Thus we might attempt to rule out the pos- sibility of the observer's suffering from a physiological disorder by adding a further hypothetical to the effect that if a physiologist were to examine him, or rather, were to seem to be examining him, it would seem to the physiologist that his patient's vision was unimpaired. But then we should require a further hypothetical to guard against the possibility that the physiologist him- self was undergoing an illusion : and so *ad infinitum*. This is not to say that the fact that some physical object fails to be observed is never to be counted as a proof that it does not exist. On the contrary, it is, under certain conditions, the very best proof obtainable. But it is not a demonstrative proof. From the fact that in the specified conditions the requisite sense-data do not occur, it does not follow logically that the physical

[1] *The Principles of Human Knowledge*, section lviii.

object in question does not exist, or that it does not have the properties it is supposed to have. In many cases this is the obvious, indeed the only reasonable, explanation of the facts; but the possibility of an alternative explanation must always remain open.

It may still be thought that this difficulty can be met by stipulating that the test for the presence or absence of the physical object is to be carried out in normal conditions by a normal observer: this is, indeed, the assumption that is tacitly made by those who maintain that to speak of any such object as existing unperceived is to imply that if one were in the appropriate situation one would be perceiving it. But this is merely a way of concealing the difficulty, not of resolving it. If we are to understand by 'normal' conditions those conditions that permit an observer to perceive things as they really are, and by a 'normal' observer one who in such conditions does perceive things as they really are, then certainly it will follow, from the fact that there is a physical object in such and such a place, that if a normal observer were there he would under normal conditions be perceiving it. But it will follow just because it is made to follow by our definition of normality. And the difficulty which we are trying to avoid will reappear immediately as the difficulty of making sure that the conditions and the observer really are, in this sense, normal. We may try to make sure by stipulating that if tests were made for every known source of abnormality, their results would all appear to be negative. But here again we shall need an infinite series of further hypotheticals to guarantee the tests themselves. Neither is it necessarily true that the sources of abnormality that are known to us are all the sources that there are. It follows that the step from descriptions of physical reality to descriptions of possible appearances cannot by this method be made formally deductive : nor, so far as I can see, can it be made so by any other.

We must conclude then, if my reasoning is correct, that the phenomenalist's programme cannot be carried through. Statements about physical objects are not formally translatable into statements about sense-data. In itself, indeed, this conclusion is not startling. It is rather what one would expect if one reflected merely on the way in which sentences which refer to physical objects are actually used. That phenomenalism has commanded so strong an allegiance has been due not to its being intrinsically plausible but rather to the fact that the introduction of sense-data appeared to leave no other alternative open. It has been assumed that since statements about physical objects can be verified or falsified only through the occurrence of sense-data, they must somehow be reducible to statements about sense-data. This is a natural assumption to make, but the result of our examining it has been to show that it is false.

(vii)

The justification of statements about physical objects

The failure of phenomenalism does not mean, however, that there is no logical connection of any kind between the way physical objects appear to us and the way they really are.[1] There may be no specifiable set of circumstances in which the fact that one does not seem to perceive a certain physical object entails that it does

---

[1] In the development of this point I am indebted to Mr. P. B. Downing.

not exist; but given that it is the kind of object that is supposed to be perceptible, it surely would follow that it did not exist if there were no circumstances whatsoever in which it would seem to be perceived. Admittedly, this premise is not one that could ever be conclusively established. Considering the manifold possibilities of illusion, there are few cases in which it even stands much chance of being true. It is a far stronger premise than one would actually require in order to be justified in concluding that some alleged physical object did not exist. Its importance consists in the fact that, in the unlikely event of its being true, the falsity of any statement which implied the existence of the physical object in question would follow as a logical consequence.

Just as a statement which implies the existence of a given physical object is not formally refuted by the fact that in a specified set of circumstances the object does not seem to be perceived, so the fact that it does seem to be perceived is not a demonstrative proof that the statement is true. And this, if I am right, applies whatever the particular circumstances may be, and however far the description of them may be extended. But now suppose it were the case that in what appeared to be the relevant setting the object would always seem to be perceived, no matter what further experiences were obtainable. Then, I think, it would logically follow that the object did exist. Once more the premise is not one that could be conclusively established: not only that but I cannot think of any instance in which there is even the least likelihood of its being true. There is no object so obtrusive that it could never under any conditions escape one's observation, even though one were placed in the right position for observing it; and this applies even to one's own body, as the possibility of anaesthesia shows. But the truth or falsity of our premise is not what is here in question. The important point is that if it were true in any given instance, the existence of a certain physical object would, on the evidence, be logically guaranteed.

What we have done, in short, is to set out a pair of limiting cases. If the argument is correct, they prove that in this matter of perception it is logically impossible for appearances to fool all the people all of the time. This is, however, consistent with anyone's being fooled in any particular instance. But if he is fooled, there will be a reason why he is fooled. I do not mean by this a causal explanation, though it is to be expected that this too will be forthcoming: I mean that the proof that he is fooled is itself to be found among the appearances. To revert to the language of sense-data, it will be found that different sense-data are obtainable from those that one would expect to be obtainable if he were right. Of course it is possible that the perceptions which seem to show up his error are themselves delusive; but they in their turn are subject to the test of further appearances. It is because this process is fluid that phenomenalism comes to grief. It is not that physical objects lurk behind a veil which we can never penetrate. It is rather that every apparent situation which we take as verifying or falsifying the statements which we make about them leaves other possibilities open. The phenomenalists are right in the sense that the information which we convey by speaking about the physical objects that we perceive is information about the way that things would seem, but they are wrong in supposing that it is possible to say of the description of any particular set of appearances that this and only this is what some statement about a physical object comes to. Speaking of physical objects is a way of interpreting our sense-experiences ; but one cannot delimit in advance the range of experiences to which such interpretations may have to be adjusted.

One way of expressing this conclusion would be to say that in referring as we do to physical objects we are elaborating a theory with respect to the evidence of our senses. The statements which belong to the theory transcend their evidence in the sense that they are not merely re-descriptions of it. The theory is richer than anything that could be yielded by an attempt to reformulate it at the sensory level. But this does not mean that it has any other supply of wealth than the phenomena over which it ranges. It is because of this, indeed, that they can constitute its justification. Accordingly, it does not greatly matter whether we say that the objects which figure in it are theoretical constructions or whether, in line with common sense, we prefer to say that they are independently real. The ground for saying that they are *not* constructions is that the references to them cannot be eliminated in favour of references to sense-data. The ground for saying they *are* constructions is that it is only through their relationship to our sense-experiences that a meaning is given to what we say about them. They are in any case real in the sense that statements which affirm or imply their existence are very frequently true.

In the end, therefore, we are brought to the unremarkable conclusion that the reason why our sense-experiences afford us grounds for believing in the existence of physical objects is simply that sentences which are taken as referring to physical objects are used in such a way that our having the appropriate experiences counts in favour of their truth. It is characteristic of what is meant by such a sentence as 'there is a cigarette case on this table' that my having just the experience that I am having is evidence for the truth of the statement which it expresses. The sceptic is indeed right in his insistence that there is a gap to be overcome, in the sense that my having just this experience is consistent with the statement's being false; and he is right in denying that a statement of this kind can be reduced to a set of statements about one's sense-experiences, that is, to a set of statements about the way that things would seem. He is wrong only in inferring from this that we cannot have any justification for it. For if such a statement functions as part of a theory which accounts for our experiences, it must be possible for them to justify it. The very significance of the theory consists in the fact that its statements can in this way be justified. It may well be thought that such an answer could have been given at the outset, without so much ado. But here, as so often in philosophy, the important work consists not in the formulation of an answer, which often turns out to be almost platitudinous, but in making the way clear for its acceptance.

CHAPTER IV

MEMORY

(i)

Habit memory and the memory of events

PHILOSOPHERS who write about memory are generally inclined to treat it as though it were analogous to perception. Though what is remembered is past, the remembering takes place in the present. It is therefore assumed that there must be some present content which gives, as it were, its flavour to a memory-experience. This present content, which is commonly thought of as a memory image, is treated as a private object, very much like a sense-datum. And just as sense-data appear to cut us off from physical objects, so these present contents of our memory-experiences appear to cut us off from the past. At this point, as we have remarked, the sceptic finds his opportunity. He argues, on grounds which we have already indicated, that since it is logically impossible that one should ever observe a past event, one can have no valid reason for believing that it occurred. Again, this argument may be met by denying the sceptic's premise. The analogy to holding that physical objects are directly perceived is to hold that we have the power of being directly acquainted with past events. But many philosophers find this answer unsatisfactory, or even unintelligible. They therefore seek other solutions. The analogy to the phenomenalist theory of perception is, as we have noted, the implausible view that statements about the past are reducible to statements about the present or future evidence that we have, or could obtain, in favour of them ; evidence in which the occurrence of memory-experiences would play a part. There is no very strict analogy to the causal theory ; but it is sometimes maintained that our trust in our memories can be justified by an inductive argument. The objection that this is no ordinary inductive argument may then lead to the conclusion that the deliverances of memory are justified in their own way. And here a parallel may be drawn with the general problem of induction. It may be argued that while the truth of any one belief which is supposed to be based on memory may be tested by reference to another, there can be no question of justifying memory as a whole : the demand for such a justification would be illegitimate.

Let us begin, as before, with the sceptic's original premise. The first point to notice is that, at best, it applies only to what may be called the memory of events. In a great many cases where one is said to remember something there is no question of one's even seeming to recall any past occurrence. The remembering consists simply in one's having the power to reproduce a certain performance. Thus, remembering how to swim, or how to write, remembering how to set a compass, or add up a column of figures is in every case a matter of being able to do these things, more or less efficiently, when the need arises. It can indeed happen, in cases of this sort, that people are assisted by actually recalling some previous occasion on which they did the thing in question, or saw it done, but it is by no means necessary that they should be. On the contrary, the better they remember, the less likely it is that they will have any such events in mind : it

is only when one is in difficulties that one tries as it were
to use one's recollections as a manual. To have learnt
a thing properly is to be able to dispense with them.

But still, it may be argued, even if one remembers
how to do things without having any conscious recollection of having done them before, or of having learned
to do them, there must be at least an unconscious
recollection. Otherwise how would one know what to
do ? But what does this 'unconscious recollection'
amount to ? Simply to the fact that one succeeds in
doing whatever it may be, with the implication that
this is the result of learning and practice. Certainly
the causes of one's proficiency include one's past experiences. The reason why we speak of remembering in
these contexts is just that we suppose ourselves to be
dealing with things that have been learned. And it
may be that these past experiences have left physical
traces which are discernible, for instance, in our brains ;
the physical mechanism of this type of memory is not
here in question. What we are concerned with is simply
the description of these processes of remembering ; and
in this the hypothesis regarding physical traces plays
no part, though it may in their explanation ; it is not
suggested that remembering how to do things actually
involves inspecting one's own brain. But neither need
it involve inspecting the past events, or any mental
representatives of the past events, which are causally
responsible for the present performance. One may say
that they are recollected unconsciously, if one means
no more by this than that one's present ability to
remember is causally dependent upon them, and so in
its way a sign of their having taken place. But it would
be much less misleading to say that they are not recollected at all.

L

Philosophers have recognized the existence of this class of cases, and they have grouped them under the heading of 'habit-memory', in contrast to 'factual-memory', or the memory of events. What they have not always realized is how far the class extends. It covers not only the instances of knowing how to do things, in which, as we have seen, it is not necessary that one should also know that anything is the case, but also a great many instances in which the knowledge displayed is classified as knowledge of fact. Suppose that I am set to answer a literary *questionnaire*, and that I have to rely upon my memory. I shall, perhaps, succeed in remembering that such and such a poem continues in such and such a way, that So-and-so was the author of such and such a book, that a given incident appears in this novel rather than in that. But none of this need involve my having any recollection of a past event. I may recall some of the occasions on which I read, or was told about, the books in question, but equally I may not. Here again, the more readily my memory functions, the less likely it is that I shall engage in any reflections of this sort. Neither is it necessary that I should entertain any images. Some people may, indeed, assist their memories by visualizing the printed page ; others, perhaps, by recalling the sound of a recitation ; but these are personal peculiarities. Others, again, just write the answers down. The image, if it occurs, is simply an *aide-mémoire* ; it does not go to constitute the memory. The proof that it is dispensable in these cases is that many people habitually dispense with it.

In the same way, a historian who remembers, for example, what the state of parties was throughout the reign of Queen Victoria, a biologist who remembers

Lamarck's version of the theory of evolution, a mathematician who remembers Pythagoras's proof of the existence of irrational numbers, a jurist who remembers a point of corporation law, need none of them be recollecting any past event; nor need they be having any images. Their remembering just consists in their getting the answer right. Whether they are helped to do so by conjuring up images, or consciously delving into their past experience, is irrelevant. Once more, the more easily they remember, the less likely it is that they will need any assistance of this sort. And here the point is not that the word 'remember' is used dispositionally, so that one can properly be said to remember things that one is not actually thinking of. It is that when such dispositions are actualized, their actualization consists in nothing more than giving a successful performance. In this sense, to remember a fact is simply to be able to state it. The power is displayed in its exercise; and such exercises need not be accompanied by anything that one would be even tempted to call a memory-experience.

(ii)

Dispensability of memory images

It is characteristic of this type of memory that it does not, except incidentally, yield knowledge of the past. Certainly, in the case of the historian, the facts which are remembered are facts about the past; but, so far as his exercise of memory goes, they might just as well not have been. His remembering them consists in his stating them correctly; it would therefore be just as much a display of memory, in this sense, if the facts that he remembered were like some scientific facts in having no specific reference to time, or if they referred to the present or even to the future ; an astronomer may remember that an eclipse of the sun will take place at some future date. And not only is this type of memory not essentially linked with knowledge of the past. There are good reasons for saying that it is not a source of knowledge at all. The exercise of it is a manifestation of knowledge. But it is not by itself a ground for the acceptance of what is known. My readiness to say, for example, that Peacock was the author of *Crotchet Castle* provides no evidence that he was the author, without some further assumption such as that I have made a special study of Peacock's work, or that I do not usually make statements of this sort unless I have checked my references. Unless there were independent reasons for believing that Peacock did write *Crotchet Castle*, my 'remembering' that he did would count for nothing. I may not myself know what these reasons are ; I may well have forgotten how I ever came to have this information. But it is only these things, which I may not remember, that give any warrant for regarding what I do remember as a piece of knowledge. In short, if remembering consists, in these instances, in giving a successful performance, what makes the performance successful must be something other than the mere fact that it is given. It is not because one remembers them that one has reason to believe that the facts are so : it is because there is reason to believe that they are so that one is entitled to say that one remembers them.

But still, it may be argued, this is not the whole story. Suppose that my reason for being sure that Peacock wrote *Crotchet Castle* is that I was reading it

only yesterday. How do I know that I was reading it
only yesterday? Because I remember doing so. Or
possibly because I find it noted in my diary. But how
do I know that words which are written down in
diaries do not spontaneously change their shape, so that
what to-day appears as 'Peacock' might yesterday have
appeared as 'Thackeray'? For all sorts of reasons.
But when they are examined it will be found that at
some point or other they all involve the fact that
someone remembers that something was so. The
observations which we use to check our memories are
interpreted in the light of hypotheses which are themselves accepted on the basis of past experience. Which
brings us back again to memory; but to memory in a
different sense from that which we have so far been
considering, the sense in which to remember something
consists in recollecting a past event. And surely in this
sense memory is a source of knowledge. The evidence
that the past event occurred is to be found in the
character of one's present memory-experience.

But what exactly is this experience? The usual
assumption is that it consists primarily in the presence
of a distinctive sort of image. Thus, Hume's analysis
of memory is that it is simply a matter of having an
idea, by which he means an image, which is a copy
of some previous sense-impression. These ideas of
memory are distinguished from impressions by the fact
that they are fainter, and from ideas of imagination by
the fact that they are livelier.[1] Russell, who in this as
in other cases is inclined to follow Hume, sees, however,
that this talk of faintness and liveliness is inadequate.
According to him what makes the image a *memory*
image is its being accompanied by a feeling of

[1] *A Treatise of Human Nature*, Book I, Part I, section iii.

familiarity.[1] Assuming, as they both do, that the past event, or experience, which is remembered, cannot itself be present to the mind, they infer that something else must be ; and an image then seems to be the only candidate.

Let us, however, look more closely at the facts. It is plausible to make the presence of an image a necessary feature of this type of memory, so long as one considers only visual examples, that is, so long as one confines one's analysis to the recollection of things seen. But what of the other senses ? I remember speaking to a friend this morning on the telephone but I do not have an auditory image either of his voice or of my own. If I have any image at all in such a case, it is likely to be visual ; a picture of my friend seated by his telephone, and possibly also of myself ; in short, a picture of something that I did not actually see. But it very often happens that one remembers such conversations without having images of any kind whatever. In the same way, I remember that a moment ago I ran my hand over the surface of my writing-table : I remember how it felt in the sense that I can give a description of the feeling, but I do not have any tactual image of it. And even in the case where one remembers something that one has seen, there need not always be a present image. If I am asked whom I met at the party to which I went last night, I may answer without hesitation that So-and-so and So-and-so were there, without having any accompanying images of their faces. I may be able to obtain such images, if I make the effort, but I can very well remember what went on, I can give an account of the party, without having any images at all. Here once again, the better one's

[1] *The Analysis of Mind*, Lecture IX.

memory functions, the more readily one replies to the question as to what took place, the greater is the likelihood that no images intervene.

Moreover, even when there is an image, it appears to play only an auxiliary rôle. To begin with, it does not greatly matter what qualities it has. Though taken by some to be a copy of the scene which it helps one to remember, it may in fact bear very little resemblance to it. Not everybody is a very good visualizer : and even the images obtained by those who are will tend to be schematic ; they will rarely, if ever, reproduce in every detail the forms and colours of the remembered scene. But so far as one's ability to remember goes, a 'bad' image may be just as serviceable as a good one. It is not as if one carefully inspected the image, as an intelligence officer inspects an aerial photograph, in the hope of finding in it a faithful reproduction of the past. It is rather as if the image were transparent : one has the impression of looking at the original picture *through* it, in much the same way as one grasps the sense of words through handwriting or print. There is this difference, however, that whereas, if the handwriting is very bad, it becomes difficult, if not impossible, to understand what it is meant to express, the image can be as fuzzy as you please without any detriment to the memory which it assists.

Neither is this simply a question of psychology. As a matter of logic, however faithful the image, it cannot be merely because of its fidelity that it signifies a past event. Considered simply as an object, it has the properties that it has : such and such an outline, such and such details, such and such a degree of vividness. Now it may be that this collection of properties bears a close resemblance to the collection of properties which characterized some previous occurrence, but this is not something that is detectable in the image taken by itself. Even if the image had, as it were, written on it its claim to be a copy of something else, this would, apart from the interpretation that we give it, be only one further feature of its appearance, an extra piece of decoration. And the same applies if one tricks the image out with feelings of familiarity. Unless these so-called feelings of familiarity are taken as comprising a judgement to the effect that something like this occurred before, they merely put an aura round the image, an aura which is no more capable than its other features of signifying anything else. In sum, a present image can refer to a past occurrence only in so far as it is so *interpreted*. But if a faithful image can be interpreted in this way, so can an unfaithful one. As in the case of any other symbol, it is the use that we make of its qualities that matters, the construction that we put upon them, not these qualities themselves. The memory image serves its purpose just in so far as it prompts one to form an accurate belief about one's past experience. But then we can form such beliefs without the assistance of an image. The proof that we can is, as I have argued, that we quite often do.

There would seem, then, to be no very sharp distinction between what is called habit-memory and what we have called the memory of events. In a case of habit-memory there may be an accompanying image, as when one is assisted to remember a quotation by visualizing it in print; and conversely, one can dispense with images in remembering an event. What is decisive in both cases is one's ability to give the appropriate performance, whether it be a matter of displaying some skill, stating a fact which may or may not have reference to the past, or describing, or, as it were, re-living a past experience. These performances may be stimulated by various means, including the presence of an image ; but even in the case of the recollection of a past experience, these stimuli do not constitute the memory. The only thing that we have so far dis-covered to be essential is the true belief that the experi-ence occurred ; a belief which may consist in nothing more than a disposition to give a correct answer to any question as to what took place.

(iii)
In what does remembering consist?

All the same, it cannot be entirely correct to equate remembering an event with having a true belief about the past. I remember that the Battle of Waterloo was fought in 1815, but I certainly do not remember the Battle of Waterloo. One very good reason why I do not remember it is that I was not alive at the time. There is a sense, on the other hand, in which I do remember the Battle of Arnhem, even though I was not present at it. I remember hearing and reading about it. But then I also remember hearing and reading about the Battle of Waterloo. What is the difference which makes it correct to say that I remember the one but not the other ? Only, it seems, that in the case of the Battle of Arnhem, the experiences which I remember having were roughly contemporaneous with the event. One speaks of remembering an event primarily in the case where one actually witnessed it ; but in a deri-vative sense one can also be said to remember it if one witnessed some of its immediate effects.

Accordingly, it may be suggested that remembering an event is just a special instance of the sort of habit-memory which consists in remembering a fact. To remember an event is to be disposed to state a fact about the past, but not just any fact about the past : it must be a fact which one has oneself observed, either straightforwardly or, as it were, at second hand. What differentiates the memory of events from other memories of fact is that it ranges only over one's own previous experience. This does not mean that one remembers only one's past experiences, in the sense that one always puts oneself into the picture which one's recollection forms. One may do so, or one may not. The emphasis in memory may fall either on the situation of which one was in fact a witness, or on one's own feelings and attitude as a spectator. Very often the memory covers both. But even if one does not come into the picture, one must at least have provided the frame. In a looser sense we may be said to remember events which we have not personally witnessed, as in the example given above. But this is only an extension of the primary usage, according to which our recollection of events is limited to what we have experienced. This restriction provides a necessary condition for an event to be remembered : apart from it, the sufficient conditions are to be found in the analysis of habit-memory which we have already given.

This is an attractive suggestion, but it is open to two fatal objections. In the first place, it may be argued that the limitation to one's past experience is not necessary, on the ground that it is at least conceivable that one should recollect an event which one has not in fact experienced. And, secondly, it may be argued

that even if this is a necessary factor, its combination
with the others is not sufficient, on the ground that it
is possible to believe truly that one has had a certain
experience, without remembering it; from which it
follows that remembering it cannot simply consist in
holding the true belief.

In envisaging the possibility of recollecting an event
which one has not in fact experienced, I am not now
thinking of the cases where one's recollection is delusive.
This raises a quite different problem, into which we
shall enter later on.   I am thinking rather of the
abnormal cases in which people claim to remember the
experiences of others ; cases of alleged co-consciousness,
or cases in which people profess to have 'recaptured'
the experiences of the dead. It may be that the evidence
for such phenomena is very dubious, but for the
purpose of the present argument it does not matter
whether we accept these claims or not. The mere
fact that we can consider whether to accept them
shows, it may be argued, that the power of remembering experiences which were not one's own, in
exactly the same way as one remembers one's own
experiences, is at least to be admitted as a logical
possibility.

So strong, however, is our tendency to make the
restriction to one's own experience a necessary condition for the recollection of events, that we may be
reluctant to allow even these abnormal cases to constitute a possible exception to the rule. Thus, admitting
it to be a fact that people do sometimes seem to have
an accurate recollection of the experiences of others,
that they seem to remember them as if they were their
own, the inference which is sometimes drawn is that
they really were their own. Their possession of this

unusual power is appealed to as a proof of reincarnation. But even if we admit the facts, this method of describing them is not forced upon us. Rather than accept the hypothesis of a single person's inhabiting a series of bodies, which many would regard as preposterous, if not wholly unintelligible, we may maintain that these so-called memories are not memories at all, just on the ground that one cannot remember experiences that one has never had. Or, finally, it may be allowed that they are indeed memories, but memories of experiences which were not one's own. I am not now interested in deciding which of these three courses would be the best to take. My point is only that if it be admitted, as I think it must be, that the third course would be open to us, it follows that the restriction of the memory of events to the field of one's past experience is not logically necessary.

The same point may be illustrated by a less far-fetched example. It sometimes happens that people under hypnosis are able to remember things which they were not consciously aware of at the relevant time. Owing to some psychological impediment, a person may fail to see something that is staring him in the face. Subsequently, however, when he is hypnotized, he is able to describe it. This is generally taken as a proof that he really did see it in the first place. It is assumed that one can have experiences of which one is not conscious at the time that they occur. But if we do not like to make this assumption, it is open to us to take a different course. We can admit that the presence of the object left some physical trace upon the man, but still deny that he ever underwent the experience of seeing it; and from this it will follow that what he displays under hypnosis is the memory of

an experience which he never actually had. Again, I
do not wish to argue that this is the best way of accounting for the facts: all that is here required is the
admission of its possibility.

Such an admission may come more easily once it is
recognized that to hold a true belief about an event in
one's past experience is not sufficient for remembering
it. There is still a distinctive factor lacking. If some
one whose word I trust describes an incident in my past
of which he was a witness, I may be fully persuaded
that the incident occurred; if I am an inveterate
visualizer, I may even form a mental picture of it,
and this mental picture may in fact be accurate:
but still I do not remember it. For instance, I myself
remember very little about my early childhood, but
I have acquired beliefs about it which, judging by
the evidence available, may very well be true. Now
it sometimes happens that a belief of this sort trans-
forms itself into a memory. The transformation may
be uncertain. One says 'I do dimly recollect it',
being still not quite sure whether one does or not,
whether one has not been talked into 'remembering'
something that one does not really remember at all.
But it may also be that all of a sudden the event comes
back to one quite clearly. One has no doubt that one
remembers it. But what is it exactly that has happened? Not the acquisition of an image; for that
may have existed already, as an accompaniment to the
belief. Not even that the image becomes more vivid:
this may indeed happen in some cases, but it is not
essential; the process may take place without any
alteration to the image, or in the absence of any image
at all. The presence, then, of a peculiar feeling? Such
feelings do indeed occur: no doubt they are what

Russell had in mind when he spoke of the feeling of familiarity, but again they do not seem to be essential. At least I do not myself detect their presence on every occasion on which I exercise my recollection of a past event.

Perhaps the correct answer is that there is no one thing that is universally present in every such instance of remembering. Sometimes it is a matter of one's having an especially vivid image; sometimes, with or without an image, there is a feeling of familiarity; sometimes there is no specific mental occurrence: it is simply then a matter of one's seriously saying 'Yes, I do remember'. There can, indeed, be said to be distinctive memory - experiences, in the sense that remembering an event, whatever form it takes, 'feels different' from merely imagining it, or believing that it occurred. But these experiences do not essentially consist in the presence of a special sort of object. There is nothing in this field that corresponds to the sense-datum, even allowing sense-data to be admissible.

Neither is it the primary function of the verb 'to remember', or its equivalents, to describe any such experiences. It would, indeed, be incorrect to say that one remembered something, unless one were in the appropriate mental attitude, however little this may in fact amount to. But in claiming to remember one is not so much describing one's present state of mind as giving an assurance that the event occurred, at the same time implying that one is in a position to know that it occurred. If we wish to rebut such a claim, we do not set out to enquire into the person's state of mind. We try to show that he is mistaken in his account of the event in question; or else we may argue that he is not qualified to offer us a guarantee, or at least not the sort

of guarantee that he professes to give us in saying ' I
remember'. The event, we may say, took place a very
long time ago ; he has a strong unconscious motive for
distorting the facts ; he seems only to be repeating
what he has heard from someone else ; he was drunk
at the time ; he was not even there. Such arguments
are not decisive. We have seen that in very exceptional
cases one might even be driven to admit that someone remembered an experience which he himself had
never had. But what might cause us to make this
admission would not be an investigation into the
person's mental state. It would be rather that we were
impressed by the facts which his ' recollection' brought
to light. The accuracy of his reports, assuming that
we had some independent means of checking them,
would outweigh the insufficiency of his credentials.
We might in the end be willing to say that he remembered the events in question because we could not see
how else he could know them. But commonly we are
not so liberal. The usage of the verb ' to remember' is
partly governed by our conception of what is memor-
able. People are not supposed to offer guarantees
unless they are qualified to make them good. They
may be lucky, but that does not absolve them. In the
case of memory, as in that of knowledge in general, it
is not always sufficient just to get the answer right.

(iv)

Memory and the concept of the past

But how, it may be asked, can one ever be in a position
to offer such a guarantee ? Why should it ever be
accepted ? To say ' I remember' is supposed, in certain

circumstances at least, to be a good answer to the
question 'How do you know?' But, if our analysis is
correct, it comes down to little more than a mere
repetition of the claim to knowledge. Merely to say
that one has had a certain experience is not to give any
reason why one's statement should be believed; and
the fact that it may in certain cases be accompanied by
images or feelings of a special kind does not, on the face
of it, make such a statement any the more credible.
Admittedly, there is the further implication that one
is in a position to know. If one's recollection is challenged in a given instance, to point out that it is the
sort of experience that one would, in these conditions,
be expected to remember, is, it would normally be
thought, to give a good answer. But how is this view
to be supported? If we had found by experience that
events of the kind in question usually had happened
when people subsequently said they had, we might be
justified in applying the general rule to this particular
case. But what experiences can we have had to justify
the general rule? Only experiences of remembering,
for which the same difficulty arises. It would appear
that the most that we are entitled to say is that statements which are expressed by the use of the past tense
are found in a very large measure to cohere with one
another. But this is formally consistent with there
never having been a past at all. So far as our analysis
has taken us, it may even be wondered how anyone ever came to attach a meaning to talking of the
past.

It is such difficulties as these that philosophers try
to sweep away by arguing that memory makes us
directly acquainted with the past. 'The pastness of
[a remembered] object', says Samuel Alexander, 'is a

datum of experience, directly apprehended.' 'The
object', he goes on to explain, 'is compresent with me
as *past*.' [1]   And Professor Broad, who takes this theory
seriously though he does not himself agree with it,
argues that the fact that an event is past is not a reason
why it should not still present itself to us.[2] To say
that an event is past is not, in his view, to say that it
does not now exist. On the contrary, he thinks that
once an event has occurred, there is a sense in which it
goes on existing for all time. It is, as it were, put in
storage ; and there is no *a priori* reason why we should
not subsequently take it out and look at it.

This view of the past is fairly common, but what
does it amount to ? What proof could there possibly
be that a past event either did or did not continue to
exist ? It is to be hoped that a great many statements
about the past are true, and also that, somehow or
other, we have good reason to believe that they are true.
And if one likes to take this as a proof of the 'reality'
of the past, well and good. But then in saying that the
past is real, one will be saying nothing more than that
these statements are true ; one will not, in any sense,
be giving an explanation of their truth. Neither does
this make it clear what can be meant by saying that
past events *continue* to exist. Perhaps just that they
are preserved in memory. But in that case to say that
they continue to exist is not to account for the possibility of their being remembered. It is just another,
and misleading, way of saying that the possibility
obtains.

Much the same objection applies to the view that
memory makes us directly acquainted with the past.

[1] *Space, Time and Deity*, vol. i, p. 113.
[2] *The Mind and its Place in Nature*, pp. 249 ff.

M

The claim that 'the pastness of a remembered object is a datum of experience' may be allowed to stand if it is intended merely as a psychological comment on the way in which our memory seems to function. It brings out the point, which we have already noted, that even when a memory-experience has a present content, in the form, say, of an image, the image does not seem to stand between us and the past; we say to ourselves, apparently of the image, 'this happened' rather than 'something like this happened'; treating the image as diaphanous, we tend psychologically to identify it with the past event. On the other hand, if this is meant to be an explanation of our ability to remember, it is completely worthless. For what conceivable proof could there be that an object which I am now recollecting is 'compresent with me as past' except just that I am now recollecting it? Here, as elsewhere, the naïve realist offers us, in the guise of an explanation, what is nothing more than a re-statement of the claim to knowledge.

But perhaps the naïve realist wishes not so much to give an explanation of our ability to remember as to make the point that there need be no question in this case of our having to justify an inference. His contention may be that some memories at least are self-guaranteeing. This position gains an unmerited plausibility from the fact that the verb 'to remember', like the verb 'to know', is used in such a way that if something is remembered it follows that it was so. To speak of remembering what never happened would be self-contradictory. This does not mean, however, that one cannot think that one remembers something which in fact never happened, that memory-experiences cannot be delusive. On the contrary, it is certain that they sometimes are. For not only are there cases in which one person's memories, or alleged memories, contradict another's, but even a single person's 'memories' may be contradictory. He may 'remember' that a given event occurred, while also 'remembering' that at an earlier time he 'remembered' that it did not. Since the event either did or did not occur, the fact that both alternatives may be remembered is also a proof that some memory-experiences are veridical,[1] though it does not enable us to decide which they are. The point which is important here is that, whichever they are, they will not differ qualitatively from those that are delusive. And even if they did so differ, the support which this might be thought to give to the naïve realist's position would not be effective. He wishes to represent the act of remembering as being, in some instances at least, a cognitive performance which bears on itself the stamp of infallibility. But we have already demonstrated that there cannot be any such performances. It may be argued that, in favourable circumstances, the fact that someone is confident that he remembers puts it beyond doubt that the relevant statement about the past is true. But whatever the character of his experience, it must always be logically consistent with it that the statement in question should be false.

The remaining argument in favour of saying that we are directly acquainted with past events is that this alone explains how we come to have a conception of the past. But once more the explanation is spurious. As we have already remarked, the fact that an object was presented to us, with the words 'I am past' stamped, as it were, upon it, could not in itself give rise to any

---

[1] Assuming, of course, that there has been a past.

conception of the past at all. Unless the device, whatever it may be, is interpreted as referring to the past, it
is nothing more than a decorative addition to the object.
But if we are to interpret it as referring to the past,
our conception of the past must be independent of it.
Moreover, this conception cannot in any case have
arisen *from* the exercise of memory. For we have seen
that whatever the content of a memory-experience, it
acquires its reference to the past only through being
so interpreted. But from this it follows that the
identification of anything as a memory presupposes an
understanding of what is meant by being past. And if
this understanding is presupposed by memory, it cannot be founded on it. Psychologically it may arise
with the exercise of memory, but that is another
question.

In any case, if we insist on looking for a 'simple
idea', in Locke's sense, from which to derive the
complex idea of memory, it is not difficult to find one.
It can, I think, plausibly be maintained that the relation
of temporal precedence is 'given' to us in experience.
As a matter of empirical fact, one can see or hear A-
following-B, in the same immediate fashion as one can
see A-to the left of-B. And this relation of temporal
precedence, coupled with the notion of the present,
which may be defined ostensively, is all that is required
to yield the concepts both of the past and of the future.
Defining the present as the class of events which are
contemporaneous with *this*, where *this* is any event that
one chooses to indicate at the given moment, one can
define the past as the class of events which are earlier
than the present, and the future as the class of events
which are later than the present. This brings out also
the important point that events are not in themselves

either past, present, or future. In themselves they
stand in relations of temporal precedence which do not
vary with time ; if one event is ever earlier than another,
it is always so. Or rather, since the position of events
in time is fixed by their temporal relations, it makes no
sense to apply temporal predicates to their possession
of these relations themselves. What varies is only the
point of reference which is taken to constitute the
present. Every past event has been at different times
both present and future ; every future event will be
present and then past ; and every present event has
been future and will be past. But these facts are not
a source of contradiction, as some philosophers have
supposed : nor are they an excuse for nonsensical talk
about a multiplicity of temporal dimensions. The explanation of them is just that the point of present reference, by which we orient ourselves in time, the point
of reference which is implied by our use of tenses, is
continuously shifted. It is this shift of the point of
reference in the direction of earlier to later, not any
change in the temporal relationship of events, that
constitutes the passage of time. 'Le temps ne s'en va
pas, mais nous nous en allons' is not only a good
epigram ; it is a piece of accurate analysis.

This logical subordination of the idea of the passage
of time to that of temporal succession should be enough
to make the notion of the past, and so of memory,
respectable to those who like to see their empirical
concepts straightforwardly grounded in experience. I
do not suggest, however, that this is how the concept
of the past is actually acquired. Genetically, it may
very well be that one does not first form a concept of
the relation of temporal precedence, and then extra-
polate it to events which are beyond the range of one's

immediate experience. It seems to me more likely
that the understanding of what it is for an event to be
past develops *pari passu* with the understanding of the
use of the past tense. It may be objected that in order
to understand the use of the past tense one must already
have a conception of the past; else how would one
know to what the past tense applied? But this is to
ignore the extent to which the formation of concepts is
itself a function of the use of words. Logically it is
because there can be events which are earlier than this
that we have a use for saying 'it was so'. But psychologically it may be that we first acquire the habit of
saying 'it was so' in a certain class of present situations,
and only later identify the reference of such phrases
with events which are earlier than this.

(v)

Concerning the analysis of statements about the past

However these psychological questions are to be settled,
the logical difficulty remains. Assuming that we somehow become capable of understanding statements which
are intended to refer to the past, what possible means
have we of verifying them? We can note that they
corroborate one another, but can we go any further
than this? Is it not logically impossible that we should
discover, by direct inspection of the past, whether any
one of them is true? Memory would seem to be our
only resource, and it has been shown that memory does
not furnish us with any such power. But then what
reason can we have for believing in the occurrence of
any past events? We may have reason for believing
in the occurrence of events which some practical

difficulty prevents us from observing; but it is requisite that they should at least be theoretically
observable.

It is their acceptance of this argument that has led
some philosophers to identify statements which are
ostensibly about the past with statements which are
ordinarily taken as referring to the actual or possible
evidence on which our beliefs about the past are, or
might be, founded; that is, to statements which, on
the face of it, are not about the past at all, but about the
present and future. Rather than conclude that the
statements by means of which we try to refer to the
past are all of them unwarranted or, worse still,
nonsensical, these philosophers prefer to hold that they
do not mean what they seem to mean. By construing
them as referring to the present or future evidence that
is, or might be made, available, they think that they
at least make sure that they are capable of being verified.

Apart from this one advantage this view would
seem, however, to have nothing to commend it. To
begin with, it makes the meaning of statements which
are expressed in the past tense remarkably unstable. For
with the passage of time the range of the evidence
which is supposed to be within our reach will be continually changing. The events which it was within my
power to observe when I began to write this paragraph
have already disappeared into the past. So the interpretation of all the statements in the analysis of which
a description of these events figured will have to be
revised; the description of these events will have to
be replaced by a description of whatever present or
future events are regarded as evidence for *them*; and,
as they too fall into the past, the revised version will
constantly have to be revised again. It will follow

also, what we have already found to be objectionable, that sentences in the past and present tenses cannot express the same statement.   I describe to-day's weather by saying that the sun is shining; but if to-morrow I say 'the sun shone yesterday' I am taken to be referring not to what I now express by saying 'the sun is shining', for that will be inexpressible, but to what one will find if one looks up the records in a meteorological office, or reads the newspaper, or con-sults one's own or other people's recollections.   The possibility that these records are deceitful does not arise, except in so far as they may contradict each other, or may be contradicted by further evidence.   At any given moment, the truth or falsehood of a statement about an earlier event depends entirely on the evidence that may thenceforward be discoverable.   If from a certain time onward all the available evidence will go to show that such and such an event has occurred, then, on this view, it will follow that it really has occurred. To deny that it had occurred would simply be to predict that there would be a breakdown in the run of the favourable evidence; that it was at some later moment going to point the other way.   We are thus brought to an entirely pragmatic conception of the use of language.   Except in so far as they describe what one is actually observing — a fleeting performance, since the facts do not stay on record — the indicative use of sentences is to announce our expectations of the future.   The truth or falsehood of what they express is merely a matter of the extent to which these expecta-tions are capable of being fulfilled.

   Now it is certainly true that if, from a given moment onwards, all the available evidence goes to show that a certain event has occurred, no one who lives at any

subsequent time will have any reason to suppose that
it did not. But to allow this is surely not to allow that
the statement that the event occurred is formally entailed by the evidence. The possibility that the evidence is deceptive must remain open ; and this not only
in the sense that further evidence may fail to corroborate it. It must be at least conceivable that the
event did not in fact occur, even though from the time
at which the question is raised all the evidence that
will ever be forthcoming goes to show that it did.
Not only for emotional, but also for logical reasons,
we wish to deny that it is possible, by a suitable adjustment of the evidence, literally to manufacture the past.
The fact that the argument leads to this result should
make us suspect that its premises are faulty. Is this
really the only interpretation of statements about the
past that allows them to be verifiable ?

If it is thought to be so, it is because of the assumption that once an event is past it is inaccessible : what
is past is past and there can be no returning to it. But
is it so certain that one can have no access to the past ?
We have already remarked that, in view of the fact that
light and sound take time to reach us, there is a ground
for saying that a great many, perhaps the majority, of
our perceptions are perceptions of past events. But
this, it will be argued, is beside the point. If our
acceptance of certain physical theories, combined with
a predilection for the language of naïve realism, induces
us to say that we perceive the past, this will just be
the way that we have chosen to describe, or to account
for, a certain set of observations. By adopting such
hypotheses as that light and sound waves have a finite
velocity, we come to interpret our experiences in such
a way that a difference is established between their time

order and the time order of the physical events with which they are supposed to bring us into contact. In a rather simpler fashion, we might decide to say that to watch a news-reel in the cinema was an instance of observing the past. But the only way in which we can come to attach a meaning to any such locutions is through the application of some scientific theory, which one accepts on the basis of one's past experiences. And whatever tricks we may be able to play with the dating of physical events, our past experiences are not recapturable. Once they are gone, they are gone for ever.

But what is it that prevents one from recapturing a past experience ? With the progress of science, why should not a time machine be constructible which would enable us to travel in time, as we already succeed in travelling in space ? Why should one not literally relive the scenes of one's childhood, or, for that matter, enjoy in advance the experiences of one's old age ? It may not be technically feasible, but surely the possibility can at least be envisaged. Has it not, indeed, already been envisaged by writers of science fiction ? The answer to this is that there is no difficulty at all in supposing that one can have experiences which are exactly like the experiences of one's childhood : one can conceive of their being obtained through hypnotism, or the use of drugs ; there is no need to have recourse to anything so dubious as a time machine. But they still would not be the same experiences ; and the reason why they would not be the same is just that they would occur at a different date. Even if it were possible to have one's life over and over again, in the sense that whenever one reached a certain age one would proceed to undergo a series of experiences which

were qualitatively the same in every detail as those that
one had undergone since birth, this still would not
constitute a literal recapture of the past. One term
of the cycle would be necessarily different from
another. There is, therefore, no possibility of travelling
in time. To travel in space is to be at different places
at different times ; but the idea of being at different
times at different times is simply nonsensical. One can
imagine being projected back into the eighteenth
century, in the sense that from a given moment onwards
one would have only such experiences as would be
appropriate to that period of history ; but still they
could not be identical with the experiences that anyone,
oneself or another, had actually had before. For
inasmuch as they would succeed one's present experiences, they could not also precede them. To assign to
one and the same event two different places in the same
time order is self-contradictory.

Thus the reason why the past cannot be recaptured
is just that nothing is allowed to count as our recapturing it. It is a necessary fact that if one occupies
the position in time that one does at any given moment,
one does not at that moment also occupy a different
position. If one event temporally precedes another,
an experience which is strictly simultaneous with the
second of these events cannot also be strictly simultaneous with the first. So, if observing a past event is
taken as requiring one to have an experience which is
earlier than any experience that one is actually having,
it is a necessary fact that one cannot observe a past
event.

But from the fact that one cannot now observe an
event which took place at an earlier date, it does not
follow that the event itself is to be characterized as

unobservable.[1]   We must distinguish here between
things which are unobservable in themselves, in the
sense that to talk of anyone's observing them is contradictory or nonsensical, and things which are unobservable by a given person, because of the situation in
which he happens to be placed.   We are not accustomed
to regard events which are occurring at a different
place from that in which we happen to be as being
for that reason unobservable.   Yet it is necessarily true
that, being now where I am, I cannot make any of the
observations which would require me to be somewhere
else.   It is true that I can change my position in space,
whereas I cannot change my position in time : but to
travel in space takes time, so that I cannot observe what
is now going on elsewhere ; the best that I can do is
put myself into a position to observe what will be going
on there at some future date.   It is indeed conceivable
that I should now be somewhere else ; it is not a
necessary fact that I am where I am.   But then is it not
conceivable that I should have lived at a different time ?
When people say, for example, that they would like to
have lived in Ancient Greece, it is certainly not obvious
that the wish that they express is self-contradictory.
The question is difficult because it is not at all clear
what is required for the preservation of one's personal
identity.[2]   Our imagination, which allows us to roam
freely about space, is also equal to the idea of a certain
amount of transposition in time, but when the period
in which it seeks to place us is extremely remote, there
is an inclination to say that one would not in that case
be the same person.   But even if it were self-contra-

---

[1] I have already developed this argument in a paper called 'Statements about the Past', published in the *Proceedings of the Aristotelian
Society*, 1950–51, and reprinted in *Philosophical Essays*.
   [2] *Vide* Chapter V, sections i and ii, for a discussion of this problem.

dictory, as I do not think it is, to say of any event, which is in fact past though not described as being so, that I, being the person that I am, am now observing it, it still would not follow that the event itself was unobservable. The position is different if the event is described as being past, but then this is not a description of the event itself but only an indication of the speaker's temporal relation to it.

This is, indeed, the important point. The mistake which is made by those who think themselves obliged to turn statements about the past into statements about the present and future is that of supposing that a difference in the tense of an indicative sentence invariably makes a difference to the factual content of the statement which it expresses. It does make a difference in the cases where the tense is the only means employed for dating the event referred to. Clearly, if I now say that the sun is shining, I am making a different statement from that which I should be making if I were to say that the sun shone yesterday, or that it will shine to-morrow. But in all such cases one could convey the same information by making the dates explicit in a way that did not essentially involve the use of tenses, or of other temporal demonstratives such as the words 'yesterday' or 'to-morrow'. Instead of using the present tense and leaving it to be understood from the context what date I am referring to, I could record the occurrence of sunshine at a certain place on August 20th, A.D. 1955. And then it makes no difference to the content of the record whether it is the expression of a prediction, a contemporary observation, or an act of memory. If I am speaking before the event I shall make use of the future tense, and if I am speaking after the event I shall make use of the past tense, but the fact which I describe will be in either case the same. In such an instance, the substitution of one tense for another serves to give a different indication of the temporal position of the speaker with respect to the occurrence to which he is referring, but the meaning of the sentence is not otherwise affected. The truth or falsehood of a statement which purports to describe the condition of the weather at a given date is quite independent of the time at which it is expressed. By combining a description of the event in question with a reference to the temporal position of the speaker, the use of tenses brings together two pieces of information which are logically distinct. It does this in an economical fashion, but it is not indispensable. Either piece of information could perfectly well be given in a language that contained no tenses at all. The temporal position of the speaker, relatively to the event described, which is shown by this use of the present, past, or future tense, could itself be characterized by being explicitly assigned a date.

We come then to a conclusion which we have already anticipated in remarking that events, considered in themselves, are neither present, past, or future. For it follows from this that considering only the factual content of a statement, irrespective of the time at which it is expressed, no statement is as such about the past. It may describe an event which is earlier than the occasion of its being expressed, and it may itself refer to this temporal relationship. But both the characterization of the event and the account of its temporal relationship to a particular occasion of its being described are pieces of information that could be given at any time. The fact that they are given at one time rather than another may bear upon the strength of the

reasons that we at present have for accepting them, but
it has no bearing on their content. Thus, the analysis
of a given statement is not affected by the question
whether the statement is delivered before, or after, or
simultaneously with the event to which it refers. From
which it follows that inasmuch as the verifiability of a
statement depends only on its meaning, a statement
which is verifiable when the event to which it refers is
present is equally verifiable when the event is future
or past.

The importance of this argument is that it pre-
serves us from having to accept an implausible analysis
of statements about the past ; it shows that there is no
need for us to try to convert them into statements about
the present or future. Even so, it may be objected, it
does not take us very far. Let it be granted that statements about the past are verifiable in themselves. The
fact remains that we, who happen to be living at a later
time, are not, and could not be, in a position to verify
them. It may, or may not, be conceivable that we
should have occupied a different position in time. We
have to accept the fact that we occupy the position that
we do : and, this being so, there is no means now
available to us of observing an event which would be
accessible to us only if we occupied an earlier position.
As has already been shown, there is nothing even that
would count as our returning to the past. But this
means that we are still confronted with the problem
of showing how we can ever be justified in accepting
statements which purport to describe these past events.

It might seem that if we are to be justified at all it
must be by an inductive argument. We have, indeed,
already established that one of the conditions which is
ordinarily required for an inductive argument to be

valid can be met; the conclusion is not as such unverifiable. But what is the evidence on which the
argument would be based ? There is not even a single
instance in which anyone has actually observed the
conjunction of a present and a past event; or rather,
if there are said to be such instances, as in the cases
where an event like a solar eclipse is calculated to be
past at the time when it is observed, it is only in virtue
of some scientific hypothesis which, as we have noted,
would not itself be justifiable unless we had independent
reasons for believing in the existence of certain past
events. One may argue that if it is reasonable to expect
a given process to continue into the future it must also
be reasonable to infer that it grew out of the past. If
'change and decay in all around I see', there must be
something that things have changed out of, as well as
something that they are changing into. Not every
process can start in mid-career, like Minerva springing
fully armed from the head of Jove. But to speak of a
process starting in mid-career is to imply that processes
of its kind normally have antecedent phases. The
change that I am said to see is mostly change that I
remember. Our right to conceive of current processes
as extending in both temporal directions is itself based
upon our knowledge of the past. There would appear
then to be no escaping from this circle. Any attempt
to justify a statement about the past by an inductive
argument is found at some point to involve the assumption that some statement about the past is true.

Indeed, it is obvious that this must be so. Since no
event intrinsically points beyond itself, our reason for
linking a later with an earlier event, for assuming that
the one would not in the given circumstances have
occurred unless the other had preceded it, must lie in

our acceptance of some general hypothesis; that is to say, we account for the later event by correlating it with the earlier. The hypothesis which gives us our warrant for doing this will itself be supported by evidence for which other hypotheses will provide a backing in its turn. There may thus be no statement about the past that one is not, if one accepts it, prepared to justify; even if the justification sometimes consists in nothing more than an appeal to memory, an appeal the force of which lies in the assumption that people are commonly in a position to know about the events which they claim to remember, that their reports of these events are to be trusted; and this is again a general assumption for which evidence can be adduced. So one statement about the past is used to justify another; but still there is no independent means of justifying them all. There is not, because there could not be. To obtain this justification one would have to be able to recapture the past in a way that has been shown to be logically impossible.

It does not follow, however, that we must renounce any claim to knowledge of the past. Historians cannot perform impossible feats of temporal projection; they cannot make a later event coincide with, or precede, an earlier event in the same time-series; but still there are canons of historical evidence. One authority is checked against another; psychological and economic laws are brought into play: in a considerable number of cases the evidence attains a strength which makes it proper to say that some statement about an earlier event is known to be true. Not that any such statement will be logically entailed by the evidence, except in such cases as the evidence is taken as including general propositions which themselves will draw their support from

N

statements about the past. For instance, the statement that the earth is millions of years old is supported by a wealth of geological evidence; it would not be incorrect to say that we know it to be true. There are, however, people who for religious reasons prefer to believe that the earth came into existence only a few thousand years ago but already bearing perceptible signs of age. We may say that this is a silly view: if we know the other to be true, we know it to be false, but it is formally compatible with the evidence. Even the view that the earth and all its inhabitants had come into existence just at this moment would not be formally inconsistent with anything that one could now observe. What it would contradict would be the accepted interpretations and explanations of the phenomena; it would be an arbitrary denial of them, and all the more irresponsible in that it would furnish us with no other means of accounting for subsequent events. The case for the scientifically orthodox explanations is that they do explain.

Still it is logically conceivable that they are false. And if anyone chooses to make this a reason for withholding even a provisional judgement on them, if anyone chooses, in particular, to maintain that our being unable to recapture any past experience leaves it an entirely open question whether any statement about the past is true, I do not know what more there is left to say to him: any more than I know what there is to say to someone who maintains that the fact that scientific hypotheses go beyond their evidence deprives us of any right to form expectations of the future. We can say that he is irrational; but this will not worry him; our standard of rationality is just what he objects to. Our only resource is to point out, as we have done, that the proof that he requires of us is one that he makes it logically impossible for us to give. It is, therefore, not surprising that we cannot furnish it : it is no discredit to the proofs which we do rely on that they do not imply that we can achieve the impossible ; it would be a discredit to them, rather, if they did.

(vi)
The past and the future : memory and precognition

Allowing, then, that we have some knowledge of the past, we may conclude that part of it is yielded by memory. It may even be suggested that memory is the primary source of all such knowledge, that it supplies the foundation which other forms of record only extend and supplement. But our analysis of memory has gone to show that this is incorrect. If the fact that one seems to remember an event is a good reason for believing that it occurred, it is only because there is independent evidence that when someone says that he remembers something the chances are that it was so. It is not simply a matter of one's memories being self-consistent, or of their agreeing with what other people say that they remember ; this counts for something, but so even more does written evidence, or the deductions that we make from scientific laws. It is true that we rely on memory for some of the data on which these laws are based, but then these data are checked in turn by further evidence. In sum, the part played by memory is important but not decisive. If we were all to lose our memory of events, it would be harder for us to reconstitute the past, but not impossible ; the cross-checking of written and other physical records, the utilization of the scientific theories which they supported, could suffice. We should still need habit-memory, for without it the evidence would be no good to us; we should not know how to interpret it. But this means only that we retain what we have learned in the form of a disposition to perform successfully. It has been shown that it need not involve the recollection of any past event.

If philosophers have been inclined to over-weight the contribution of memory to knowledge, the reason may be that they have not wholly rid themselves of the fallacious conception of memory as a kind of internal camera, a camera which is unique in having the magical power of directing its lens upon the past. It is not thought that there is any corresponding camera for recording the future. The indulgence shown to memory is not normally extended to precognition: it is assumed that any evidence which would tend to show that precognition does occur can be rejected out of hand; or at least that it must somehow be explained away. Yet there is no *a priori* reason why people should not succeed in making true statements about the future in the same spontaneous way as they succeed, by what is called the exercise of memory, in making true statements about the past. In neither case is their state of mind important; all that matters is that they get the answers right without having had to work them out. Some people do claim that they can achieve this with respect to certain future events, just as we all can with respect to certain past events, but their achievements, so far as I have been able to learn, are not particularly impressive. The argument against precognition is, therefore, not logical but empirical; the evidence in favour of its occurrence is still very weak.

A motive for regarding it with suspicion is also that it would be difficult to explain scientifically. We are accustomed to think of experiences leaving their shadow behind them, in the form, perhaps, of traces in our brains, but it is hard to envisage any physical mechanism by means of which coming events could cast their shadows before. Still, if the fact were established, it is to be presumed that some scientific explanation for it would eventually be found.

Just as the myth of the internal camera leads people to say that the past must still exist in order to be remembered, so there is a tendency for them to think that if future events were precognized, they would have to exist already. Then some take this apparent contradiction to be a logical argument against the possibility of precognition and others try to get round it by making the nonsensical assumption that the future may be present in a second dimension of time. But the difficulty is quite illusory. To precognize something is to know, not what *is* happening, but what *will* happen, just as to remember something is, in this sense, to know, not what is happening, but what *has* happened. To argue that if one were to precognize a future event it would be not future at all, but present, is just as absurd as to argue that if one remembers a past event, it is present and not past: unless the event really were future there would be no question of one's *pre*-cognizing it. In general, there is as little reason to say that the future already exists as there is to say that the past still exists; as little and as much. If to say that the past exists can be taken as a way of saying that a number of statements about the past are true, then to say that the future exists can be taken as a way of saying that a number of statements about the future are true. But are they true already ? The question betrays a confusion of thought. Certainly the events which make such statements true have not yet occurred : what is stated is not that they have occurred but that they will. But if the statements are true at all, they are true at any time. Or rather, it does not make sense to ask at what time they are true. I may, for example, ask for the date of the next full moon and be given the true answer that it will be on Friday, September 2nd. But to ask for the date of the fact that there is (has been, or will be) a full moon on Friday, September 2nd, is to raise a nonsensical question. Dates enter into facts, in the sense that an event's occurring at a certain time may be what makes a given statement true, but facts themselves are dateless.

It is to be noted that people do not feel the same temptation to fall into the error of saying that state-ments about the past are no longer true. And one reason for this may be that they have very different pictures of the past and of the future. The past is thought of as being 'there', fixed, unalterable, indelibly recorded in the annals of time, whether we are able to decipher them or not. The future, on the other hand, is regarded as being not merely largely unknown but largely undecided. Some would indeed regard it as being wholly undecided ; and for this very reason they are reluctant to allow that any facts about it can really yet be known. Thus the future is thought to be open, whereas the past is closed. When we look backwards, the stream of history seems to flow along a single channel, but when we look forwards, there seem to be any number of courses it can take. Only, as soon as one of them is taken, the others are abolished. They remain in the picture only as shadowy 'might-have-beens'.

Whatever the psychological attractions of this way of thinking, it has no justification in logic at any point. The difference between the past and the future is that past events are earlier than those which at the instant of speaking constitute the present, and future events are later. But there is nothing in this difference to warrant the conclusion that the future is open, or undecided, or unknowable, in a way that the past is not. On the contrary, in any sense, other than its merely being past, in which the past is closed, so is the future; and in any sense, other than its merely being future, in which the future is open, so is the past. The past is closed in the sense that what has been has been : if an event has taken place there is no way of bringing it about that it has not taken place; what is done cannot be undone. But it is equally true, and indeed analytic, that what will be will be ; if an event will take place there is no way of bringing it about that it will not take place; what will be done cannot be prevented : for if it were prevented it would not be something that will be done. The future is open in the sense that from the fact that at any given moment the course of events has reached the point that it has it does not follow that it will continue in this direction rather than in that. There is only one direction that it will in fact take, but that this will be so is not deducible from any set of statements that merely describe the present condition of affairs ; there may be causal limitations, but the logical possibilities are unlimited. But in this sense the past is open also. From the fact that the course of events has reached the point that it has it does not follow that it has come from this direction rather than from that. Given a set of statements that merely describe the present condition of affairs, one can no more deduce anything about the past than one can about the future. In both cases, whatever causal limitations there may be, the logical possibilities are unlimited. It does, indeed, follow from the fact that the course of events has been just what it has that it has not been something different : but the same applies to the future. The exclusion of other possibilities follows from the fact that the course of events will be just what it will.

That the course of events will be what it will is a logical truism ; yet many people are reluctant to admit it, because they think that it commits them to some sort of fatalism. They imagine that it requires them to conceive of the future as being, like the past, already recorded in the ledger of history : and this makes them think that all activity is fruitless, since whatever it produces was bound to happen in any case. In the same way, they may object to the idea that the future can be known, on the ground that this would imply that its course was already determined, that it could not be otherwise. There are those, on the other hand, who think that if only they could foresee the future, they would be able to avoid the evils which lie in store for them. But if these evils really do lie in store for them, they will not be able to avoid them ; and if they do avoid them, they will not have been foreseen : for to say that an event is foreseen is, in this usage, to imply that it will occur. There is a sense, then, in which, if one had foreknowledge of an event, it would be bound to happen, but it is a trivial sense. It is simply that there would be a contradiction in saying that one knew what was false. Even if, without knowing anything, one succeeded in making a true statement which implied that a certain event occurred, the event

would, in this trivial sense, be bound to occur ; for if
it did not the statement would not be true. And this
applies equally whether the event is past, present, or
future. It does not follow, however, that the event is
necessitated in any but this purely verbal way. It does
not follow that it is causally determined, though it well
may be. And it does not follow, nor is it likely to
be true, that it would occur whatever else occurred.
Certainly, if an event is going to happen, then it will
occur whatever else does occur : but this is not at all
the same as saying that nothing makes any difference
to its occurrence. There may be a great many things
that would prevent it ; if it is going to happen, they
are not, but this does not mean that it would still have
happened even if they had. Thus, the recognition of
the tautology that what will be will be is not at all a
ground for concluding that our activities are futile.
They too, indeed, are what they are and their consequences will be what they will ; but it does not
follow, nor is it in general true, that whatever they were
their consequences would be the same.

So the answer to the fatalist is that his bogy is a
fraud. If his only ground for saying that an event is
fated to occur is just that it will occur, or even that
someone knows that it will, there is nothing more to
his fate than the triviality that what happens at any
time happens at that time, or that if a statement is true
it is true. His bogy would not be a fraud if he could
establish that what happens at one time must be causally
independent of what happens at another, and in particular, that the future must be independent of the
present : but this he cannot do. And, this being so,
it would seem that we have at last found a sense in
which the future is open whereas the past is closed.

Surely the difference is that while we cannot now do anything about the past, we can do something about the future. Admittedly, we cannot make the future other than what it will be any more than we can make the past other than what it was. But whereas our present actions can have no effect upon the past, they can have an effect upon the future. They can make it other than it would have been, had they not been done.

(vii)
Why cannot cause succeed effect?

This distinction which we are required to draw between the past and the future is based on the principle that cause cannot succeed effect. And I do not think that we can deny that this principle is true. It is, indeed, necessarily true. The use of the word 'cause' is such that if one event is said to be the cause of another, it is implied that it precedes, or at any rate does not succeed, the event which is said to be the effect. But while the propriety of this usage cannot be contested, it is difficult to account for. It is hard to see why one should insist on making it impossible for a later to cause an earlier event.[1]

I suppose there are many to whom the very idea of a later causing an earlier event would seem an absurdity, not just because it does violence to ordinary usage, but because they cannot conceive how something which does not yet exist could already be exerting its influence. They will admit that a thing which already

---

[1] Cf. A. E. Dummett, 'Can an Effect Precede its Cause?', *Supplementary Proceedings of the Aristotelian Society*, vol. xxviii, and my article on 'L'Immutabilité du passé', *Études philosophiques*, 1953, no. 1.

exists can bring into being something which had not
existed hitherto; it does not therefore seem to them
perplexing that a thing which does not yet exist should
be acted upon : where their imagination baulks is at
the idea of its already being an agent.

This objection is instinctively appealing, but it does
not withstand the analysis of what is meant by one
thing's acting on another : that is, assuming, as the
argument requires, that this notion of agency is co-
extensive with that of cause. For to say that *a* is the
cause of *b*, when *a* and *b* are separate events, is, in
the usage which is here in question, to imply either
that *a* is a sufficient condition of *b*, or that it is a necessary condition of *b*, or that it is both a sufficient and a
necessary condition : it may also be understood that
these relations are supposed to hold only in the presence
or absence of certain other factors which need not be
actually specified. And what is meant by saying that
a is a sufficient condition of *b* is that however the
circumstances are varied, other than those whose con-
stancy is tacitly implied, *a* would not occur without
b's also occurring ; while what is meant by saying that
it is a necessary condition of *b* is that *b* would not occur
without it. But from this it immediately follows that
if *a* is a sufficient condition of *b*, *b* is a necessary condition of *a*; indeed, these are just two ways of saying
the same thing, that *a*, as it were, carries *b* along with
it. And so also, if *a* is a necessary condition of *b*, *b* is a
sufficient condition of *a*, and if either one is a necessary
and sufficient condition of the other, the relationship is
reciprocal.

It follows then that if, as frequently happens, an
earlier event is a necessary condition of a later one, the
later event is a sufficient condition of the earlier ; if an

earlier event is a sufficient condition of the later, the
later is a necessary condition of the earlier : and in the
case, of which it is harder to find examples, in which
an earlier event is both a necessary and sufficient condition of a later event, the later event is in its turn both
a necessary and sufficient condition of the earlier one.
If, for example, it is a necessary condition of my
suffering from malaria that I should have been bitten
by the anopheles mosquito, then my suffering from
malaria is a sufficient condition of my having previously
been bitten : if my taking arsenic in the appropriate
quantities is a sufficient condition of my subsequently
dying in a certain way, then my dying in that way is
a necessary condition of my previously taking the
arsenic. I should not be taking the arsenic unless I
were about to die, just as I should not be suffering
from malaria unless I had been bitten by the mosquito.
And if, let us say, it is in certain circumstances both a
necessary and sufficient condition for a projectile to
rebound at a given angle and with a given velocity from
a wall, that it should have struck the wall from such and
such an angle and with such and such a velocity, then
its rebounding in that way from the wall is also a
necessary and sufficient condition of its striking it. It
would not have rebounded in that way unless it had
so struck it, but equally it would not have struck it in
that way unless it had been going to rebound.

Consequently, apart from the stipulation that a
cause must not succeed its effect, we would seem to
have just as much reason for believing that earlier
events are caused by later events as for believing that
they cause them. And why should we make this
stipulation ? Why among all the events which we can
discover to be necessary or sufficient conditions of

other events, should we pick out just those that happen
to be earlier than the events to which they are so
related, and give them the special name of causes? It
is not as if through being earlier they were in any
sense more efficacious. One reason which may be
offered is that the course of events is such that we are
able to make more precise inferences from earlier to
later than we can from later to earlier. There may,
for example, be more processes in nature with similar
ends but dissimilar beginnings than there are with
similar beginnings but dissimilar ends; a suggestion
which finds support in the hypothesis that the world
is growing more uniform with time. But this distinction, if it obtains, is only a distinction of degree; it
does not seem marked enough to account for our giving
causality its one-way direction.

A more promising explanation is that our notion of
causality is derived from the experience of human
action; and human action is directed towards the
future, not towards the past. But again we may ask
why this should be so. To bring something about is
to perform an action which, in the prevailing circumstances, is a sufficient condition of the event which is
said to be its result. But such actions will have
necessary conditions which precede them; and this
means that they are also the sufficient conditions of
these earlier events. Why then, in performing these
actions, should we not be said to be bringing these
earlier events about? Yet surely no one in his senses
would set himself to bring about a past event. The
only example I can think of is that of certain Calvinists,
and even this example may be fanciful. It does, however, explain behaviour which otherwise would seem
irrational. Believing, as they did, in predestination, in

the sense that their deity had saved or damned them once for all before they were even born, they were nevertheless, on religious grounds, extremely puritanical. They believed that only salvation mattered, and yet they attached great importance to their conduct, while being convinced that it could make no difference to what lay in store for them. But now suppose that they also believed that only those whom the deity had elected were capable of being virtuous. In that case, being one of the elect would be a necessary condition for being virtuous, from which it would follow that being virtuous was a sufficient condition of having been chosen one of the elect. If this was their reasoning, then the goal of their puritanism may have lain not in the future but in the past. We may suppose that they abstained from sin in order to *have been* saved.

But even if they did reason in this way, it may still be thought that they were very foolish. Surely no refinement of logic can make such conduct sensible. What could be more absurd than to take great pains to bring about something that had already happened? But is it not equally absurd to take pains to bring about something that is going to happen? No, because it is very likely that it would not happen unless we took such pains. But then the past event might not have happened either unless we were now acting in this way. To say that something would not happen but for our acting in the way we do is to say that our action is a necessary condition of its occurrence. And we have seen that, so far as this goes, the occurrence may just as well precede the action as succeed it.

This is not to suggest that it may after all be sensible to try to bring about a past event. It plainly is not. The question still is why it is not. The obvious answer, once again, is that it is part of the meaning of causative verbs, like the verb 'to bring about', that they are forward-looking. To talk of bringing about an event which had already happened would be not merely silly but self-contradictory. But the meaning that these expressions have is the meaning that they have been given. And the question why they have been given it remains. Is it to be regarded as an arbitrary procedure? Or is there some difference between the past and the future which would account for our making this distinction between them when we speak about the possible effect of our acts?

The only relevant difference that I can find is a difference in the extent of our knowledge. Normally, when one tries to bring something about, one does not know for certain that it will happen. Not that one's actions would be any the less efficacious if one did know. We have seen, in discussing fatalism, that while if someone knows that a certain event will occur, it follows that it will occur, it does not follow that it would still occur irrespectively of what anyone did. None the less, I think that if we always did know what the results of our actions were going to be, we should come to feel differently about them. Though none of their efficacy would in fact have been removed, we should not credit them with the same dynamic quality; we should regard them rather as elements in a pattern. Our attitude, even towards our own behaviour, would tend to be that of a spectator. It is because the future seems to us uncertain that we think that we must strive to bring things about. The past, on the other hand, is not unknown to nearly the same degree; and especially not the immediate past, where the events of which we might discover our present actions to be the necessary or sufficient conditions are mainly located. The reason, then, why we do not allow ourselves to conceive of our actions as affecting past events is, I suggest, not merely that the earlier events already exist but that they are, for the most part, already *known* to exist. Since the same does not apply to the future, we come to think of human action as essentially forward-moving : and this rule is then extended to all other cases of causality. Thus, our reliance on memory is an important factor in the forming of our idea of the causal direction of events. For it exemplifies our ability to take note of what has happened, with the result that while we think we know something about the future we rightly think that we know a great deal more about the past.

CHAPTER V

MYSELF AND OTHERS

(i)

What makes a person the person that he is?

IN dealing with statements about the past, we remarked that their analysis was not affected by the fact that they were expressed at times when it was no longer possible to observe the events to which they referred. The requirement that they should be verifiable was not held to entail that any particular person, whether their author or another, should in fact be capable of verifying them. If one is to have any reason for believing them one must, indeed, have access to some evidence in their favour; but such evidence need be only indirect. It is not required that one should perform the impossible feat of returning to the past.

One cannot return to the past because it is a necessary fact that if one is placed at a certain point in time, one cannot, then or subsequently, be placed at an earlier point in time. But is it also a necessary fact that one should occupy the temporal position that one does ? It would be self-contradictory to assign two different dates to any single one of my experiences; but, given only that the experience is mine, does it follow that it occurs at any particular date, or within any given period ? It must, indeed, occur at some time during the period throughout which I exist: but is it inconceivable that this period should have been different from what it actually is; that I should, for example, have been born at a much earlier, or a much later time ? This is a question which we have already raised, but so far left undecided.[1]

The answer to it depends upon what is regarded as essential to my being the person that I am ; and this is a point which it is very difficult to settle. There are philosophers, such as Leibniz, who maintain that the notion of a given individual comprises everything that is true of him. His history being what it actually is, to suppose it changed in any respect whatever would be to represent him as a different person. On this view, not only is it inconceivable that I should have lived at a different time, it is inconceivable that at any given moment I should be at a different place from that at which I am, it is inconceivable that anything should ever happen to me except what actually does ; for if any of these facts were different, it would not be myself that was being characterized, but some other, real or imaginary, person.

In support of this view it may be argued that seeing that it is in fact true that I am, for example, at this moment wearing a grey suit, it must follow that to refer to someone who is not now wearing a grey suit is not to refer to me. And in general, given that certain things are true of me, it follows necessarily that to describe a person in a way that implies that any one of these things is not true of him is not to describe me. But, while this is correct, it does not yield the desired result ; it does not prove that any given fact about me is essential to my being the person that I am. For to say that if something is true of me then it cannot also not be true of me, is not at all the same as to say that it is necessarily true of me. If I satisfy a certain description, it does follow that I cannot be identified with someone who does not satisfy it ; but this is quite different from saying that I could not but have satisfied it, that my satisfying it is a necessary fact about me. Given the information that I do satisfy it, it becomes contradictory to add that I do not ; but this does not mean that the statement that I do not satisfy it, for example, the statement that I am not now wearing a grey suit, is contradictory when taken by itself.

Once this confusion is removed, the way is clear for rejecting the view that everything that is true about a given person is essential to his being the person that he is. For what this implies is that in mentioning a person one is covertly asserting every fact about him. But not only will there be an enormous number of such facts of which one will be completely ignorant, in which case it is hard to see how one can be assumed to be asserting them, but there may be some that one actually disbelieves. Suppose, for example, that, knowing that Benjamin Disraeli was among other things an author, I believe falsely that his works include the *Curiosities of Literature*. Then, if I assert that Benjamin Disraeli wrote the *Curiosities of Literature*, it will follow either that I am not referring to Benjamin Disraeli at all but to an imaginary person, a non-existent amalgam of Benjamin and Isaac Disraeli, or that in asserting that Benjamin Disraeli wrote the *Curiosities of Literature* I am also asserting that he did not, since in mentioning Benjamin Disraeli I am implying, among all the other facts about him, that he was not himself the author of this book, but the author's son. If it is presupposed that my attempt to name Benjamin Disraeli is successful, then only the second of these consequences holds. But each of them

is patently untenable. In the second case, it will follow
not only that I am contradicting myself when I make
this false statement about Benjamin Disraeli, but that
I am covertly mentioning his father, and not only his
father but all the other persons with whom he was in
any way associated : and in mentioning these persons
I am supposed to be implying every true statement that
can be made about them. And these facts in their turn
will bring in a great number of other persons, whose
history I must also be assumed to be relating, even
though I have never so much as heard of them. The
result is that, assuming my reference to a given
person to be successful, any statement that I make
about him, whether true or false, turns out, on this
view, to include within itself an account of pretty
well the whole of human history. This conception
of personal identity is, therefore, very quickly reduced
to absurdity.

All the same, it may be objected, there must be
some essential marks by which one person is distinguished from another. I can suppose without self-
contradiction that Benjamin Disraeli wrote other books
than those that he did write ; I can suppose that he
wrote no books at all ; that he was a liberal, not a con-
servative ; that he never even concerned himself with
politics ; that he did not marry ; that he was not
raised to the peerage. Each of these suppositions is
false, but none of them is, on the face of it, self-
contradictory. But unless I get some description of
him right, what ground is there for holding that I am
referring to him at all ? The mere use of his name
proves nothing. Other people may have the same
name, and he himself might not have had it. It
is conceivable that he should have been called not

'Benjamin Disraeli' but something else.   If changing
one's name does not make one into a different person,
then one would not be made into a different person by
having a different name from the start.

But then what is essential ?   Clearly it is in no case
a necessary fact that a certain person exists.   But given
that he exists, can one make any true statement about
him that might not have been false ?   The answer to
this might seem to be that it depends upon the way in
which one describes him in the first place.   If I begin
by describing Benjamin Disraeli as the author of
Coningsby, there is a sense in which I am logically committed to asserting at least this fact about him.   That
is to say the sentence 'the author of *Coningsby* wrote
Coningsby' can be construed in such a way that the
statement which it expresses is necessarily true. But
this is not the only reasonable interpretation of it,
though perhaps the most natural.   For the fact that the
person whom I refer to by my use of the expression
'the author of *Coningsby*' does satisfy the description
is not a necessary fact.   It makes perfectly good sense
to say that the author of *Coningsby* might not have
written *Coningsby* : and this being so, such a sentence
as 'the author of *Coningsby* wrote *Coningsby*' may also
be interpreted in such a way that the statement which
it expresses is contingent.   To put it more technically,
what looks like a descriptive expression may in fact be
used not as a description but as a pointer ; and it may
still achieve its work of reference, even though the
description in question does not fit.   It is of course
necessary that the person so referred to should be in
some way identifiable, either ostensively or by the use
of some other description : and if one identifies him
only by a description, it will be inconsistent then to

deny that he satisfies it. But again it does not follow that there is any description which he *must* satisfy, in the sense that to deny that he satisfied it would be not merely to make a false statement about him but to have mistaken his identity.

To say this is, I think, merely to make the logical point that a referential expression, like a demonstrative, need not carry any description with it. And this is the warrant for Mill's view that proper names have no connotation, though not for his further inference that they are 'unmeaning marks'.[1] If they were unmeaning marks, the substitution of one of them for another could make no difference to the sense of the expressions in which they were included, and this is plainly not the case. Mill's difficulty was in seeing how they could be meaningful if they had no descriptive content : one may be able to show what a proper name refers to, but it would be a mistake to say that this was what it meant : to ask what a proper name means would be to raise a question to which there is no answer. But while referential expressions may lack descriptive content, in the sense that they cannot be replaced, without alteration of meaning, by purely descriptive phrases, there is also a sense in which they may be credited with it. They are associated with descriptions, in the sense that one cannot understand the use of any such expression unless one can pick out some describable property of the individual to which it refers. The point is only that no one such description, or set of descriptions, is uniquely privileged.

But even if no description is logically inseparable from its owner, the attachment does in a way appear to be more intimate in some cases than in others. For

¹ John Stuart Mill, *A System of Logic*, ch. 2, section v.

instance, it is not, in this sense, at all an intimate fact
about a person that at a given moment he occupies this
or that position in space. As has already been remarked, we find no difficulty in conceiving that wherever one happens to be, one might at that time have
been somewhere else. And the reason for this is, I
think, that although, as we shall presently see, the path
which people follow in space and time is a good criterion
of their identity, the mere description of a person's
spatial position is not a useful way of identifying him ;
the fact that he is so liable to change it, and that he is
unlikely, as it were, to carry on him the marks of all
the places where he has been, means that without some
further description we should have little hope of being
able to pick him out on any other occasion. It is a
useful way of identifying features of the landscape, just
because they are stable ; and this explains why, for
example, a mountain's being at a certain place is, on
the contrary, an intimate fact about it. It may make
sense to say that the mountain might have been elsewhere — I suppose it is only a contingent fact that
mountains do not move — but we have at least a very
strong inclination to say that if it were elsewhere it
would not be the same mountain, whereas we have no
such inclination to make the corresponding statement
about a person. And this is what I mean by saying
that the fact of being in a certain spatial position is
intimate in the one case, but not in the other.

A further reason why a person's spatial position is
not regarded as an intimate fact about him is that it
has, for the most part, a negligible influence upon the
formation of his character. His development may,
indeed, be conditioned by his remaining within a
certain region for a considerable period of time ; and

just because we think that he may be vitally affected by the climate of the region, or by the customs of those who inhabit it, we may be reluctant to allow that he would still have been the same person if he had spent this time in altogether different surroundings; this does not apply, however, to the fact that at a particular moment he happens to be at a particular spot. In the same way, the exact date of one's birth is not regarded, except perhaps by astrologers, as having any great influence upon the ways in which one is disposed to feel and act. Consequently, we do not find it difficult to imagine that people might be slightly older or younger than they are. On the other hand, the fact that one lives at a certain period in history has a considerable effect upon one's general outlook and behaviour. So many of one's characteristics would be likely to have been different if one had lived at a very different time that it may seem doubtful whether one would still have been the same person in any sense at all. Furthermore, the fixity of one's temporal position, the fact that the series of events which constitute one's history has a definite place in a time-order, means that referring to dates is often a useful method of identifying people. For this reason, one's situation in time, even if it is not essential to one's being the person that one is, comes to be regarded as a more intimate fact about one than the fact that one occupies at a given moment a certain position in space. I am not maintaining that properties which may be relied on for identification are invariably regarded as intimate; it is easy to find counter-examples, such as one's finger-prints, or army number. But I think that there is a strong association here at work, even though it is not invariable.

If what I have been saying is correct, it appears that

the causal and logical aspects of the question what
makes one the person that one is are not kept sharply
distinct. One's position in time is thought to be
important because of its causal connection with the
development of one's character; and one's character,
like one's physical appearance, is regarded as an
intimate feature of one's self, inasmuch as it tends to
mark one off from others. It is relevant also that both
are comparatively little subject to change, and that such
changes as occur in them are likely to be gradual, for
there is a general tendency to attach a high degree of
intimacy to properties which are in fact found to be
stable. All the same, our imagination is not entirely
limited to the facts. We understand fairy stories in
which human beings change into trees, or even into
stones, although we do not know of any cases in which
such a thing has actually happened, and indeed believe
it to be causally impossible. It is to be noted, however,
that these are not ordinary trees or stones : they are
pictured as retaining certain human characteristics, such
as the ability to feel or even to speak, even if these
characteristics are allowed to remain dormant for a
certain period of time. It is easier, too, to conceive
of a person as changing into something of a different
species, than of his having been so all along. We can
make sense of the myth in which Philomela changes
into a nightingale : but would there be any sense in
saying that she might have been a nightingale from the
start ? If such a statement were made about a historical
character, what meaning could we attach to it ? Perhaps
that it is logically, though not of course physically,
possible that a number of descriptions which are
intimately associated with the person in question
should have been satisfied by something which had the

physical properties of a bird. But when one is put to such shifts as this, it becomes very doubtful whether one has any right to claim that one is still referring to the same individual. There is a temptation to suppose that the use of the same name by itself secures identity of reference. If I start talking, say, about Napoleon and keep the name 'Napoleon' as the subject of my sentences, it may be assumed that I am still talking about him, whatever descriptions I conjoin with the name, so long as these are significant in themselves; even descriptions which are inconsistent with the most intimate facts about him. But a consideration of examples shows, I think, that such an assumption cannot be sustained.

To the question what makes a person the person that he is we can, then, answer that certain properties are after all essential; the property of having some human characteristics, perhaps also the property of occupying some position or other in space and time. But if such properties are essential, it is because the possession of them is necessary to one's being a person at all: they do not serve to differentiate one person from another. And when we come to properties which do individuate, properties such as that of being at a certain place at a certain time, or having such and such physical traits, or being the author of such and such a work, which are in fact uniquely characteristic of the person in question, we find that they are not essential. Any one of them can be denied to their owner without self-contradiction. Nevertheless, if too many are denied the reference to the owner may be lost.

To identify me is, then, to say, not what, but who I am. It is to list some of the descriptions that I satisfy, and preferably those that I satisfy uniquely. But if I

alone do satisfy them, it is as a matter of empirical
fact, not of logical necessity. Logically, they might
apply to others as well ; or they might not apply to me.
In this sense, I could be a different, even a very different
person ; but not an utterly different person. At a
certain point, what might pass for a misdescription of
me ceases to be a description, even a misdescription, of
me at all : it is no longer I that is identified. The
difficulty is that there appear to be no rules for deter-
mining when this point is reached.

A view which I have not considered is that people
are differentiated from one another, not by the possession of any special properties, but by being different
spiritual substances, or souls. And the reason why I
have not considered it is that I do not find it intelligible.
I do not see by what criterion it could possibly be
decided whether any such spiritual substances existed.
How are we to tell, for example, whether the same
soul inhabits different bodies, simultaneously or successively ? Does it ever happen that two souls get into
a single body ? Can there be an exchange of souls
from one living body to another ? There might,
indeed, be phenomena which would lead us to consider
the possibilities of co-consciousness or reincarnation ;
we might be induced to admit exceptions to the rule
of one body, one person. But then it is the phenomena
in question that would supply us with our new criteria
of personal identity. We should still have no warrant
for interpreting them in terms of the concentration, or
dispersal, or transmigration of souls : we should not
have given any meaning to talk of this kind, except as
a way of restating what we already express more
clearly by talking about persons. But the reference to
souls is intended to account for a person's being the

person that he is, not merely to record the fact that one has somehow been identified.

If it is thought to provide an explanation, the reason may be that the process of identifying by description seems inadequate : it catches the person whom it is used to identify but it does not pin him down sufficiently. The fact that I answer to certain descriptions may enable me in practice to be recognized ; but, as we have seen, it is a contingent fact ; I might not have answered to them, even though I do. One may, therefore, be tempted to infer that *I* must be something different ; a substance that merely happens to have the properties so described. Furthermore it does not seem necessary that two different people should always be descriptively distinguishable. If, for example, history were cyclical, I should have my exact counterpart in every cycle : assuming that the whole process had no beginning or end, so that we were not differently related to a uniquely describable point of origin or termination, every description that I satisfied would also be satisfied by my counterparts ; merely by the use of predicates there would be no way of differentiating between us. Even so, we should not be identical : the very posing of the question implies that we are not. If it were contradictory to speak of different things as being descriptively indistinguishable, the suggestion that history might be cyclical could not significantly be made. But while it is a fanciful suggestion, which has no likelihood at all of being true, it does not seem to be unintelligible. That I should have such counterparts would appear to be logically possible. But in that case it will follow that people can differ otherwise than through their properties. And what, then, remains but to say that they differ in substance ? Since the argument applies not only to people, but to any individual thing, it does not, indeed, establish the existence of the soul; but the proof, if it were valid, that one was at least a substance would be an important contributory step.

Now what this argument does prove is that we are not restricted to individuating by description. We can discriminate further by the use of demonstratives, taken in their actual contexts. That I differ from my hypothetical counterparts is shown by the fact that in using the word 'I' I point to *this*, while they do not. In the same way I, alone among us, am living *here* and *now*. Descriptions of time and place will not divide us: for *ex hypothesi* each of us will stand in the same spatial relations to objects of exactly the same kind and in the same temporal relations to exactly similar events. It will be true of each of us also that he says that his use of the word 'I' points to what he indicates by saying 'this'. But the reference will be different in every case. It is a difference which defies description, just because it is not a difference of properties, not even of spatio-temporal properties unless these are made to include a reference to some point which is demonstratively identified. The use of a demonstrative on a given occasion *shows* what is being referred to: but if we are asked to say *what* is being referred to, we can reply only by giving a description; a description which normally does individuate but conceivably might not.

But does this give us any warrant for talking about substances? I do not think that it does. It seems to me, on the contrary, that philosophers have fallen here into the mistake of supposing that because referential expressions are not used to describe properties they must be used to describe something else; and substances are then brought in to fill the gap. But the truth is that they do not owe their meaning to their describing anything at all. I call them referential expressions just because their use is demonstrative and not descriptive. In an actual context, one can, as it were, produce what they refer to : but if we have to identify it by description, then we can do no more than instance some of its properties ; for there is nothing else to be described. But what is it that has the properties? Surely it must be something, even if there is nothing that one can say about it ; so that one is reduced, like Locke, to speaking of it as 'something we know not what'.[1] But what is the sense of this question? What possible ways could there be of answering it? In favourable circumstances one can produce the object that one is referring to ; and that is one form of answer. Or one can give a description of it, which is necessarily a listing of its properties. No other possibility remains.

(ii)
General criteria of personal identity.
Must they be physical?

At this point it may be objected that since various descriptions apply to the same thing, or person, there must be something that, as it were, holds them all together. It was one and the same man, Napoleon Bonaparte, who won the Battle of Austerlitz and lost the Battle of Waterloo. But in what sense was he the same ? What is it that makes a set of descriptions, which are logically independent of one another, into descriptions of the same person ?

[1] *Essay Concerning Human Understanding*, Book II, ch. 23.

This is a different question from that which we have so far been considering. We have found that, apart from the contingent fact that certain things may be true of him alone, there is nothing that especially makes a person the person that he is. But it remains possible that there are general criteria of personal identity, criteria that must be satisfied if we are to be entitled to say of any two events that they are events in the same person's history. Indeed, it would seem that there have to be such criteria if our talk of persons is to have any meaning at all. And if we can discover them, we can also give an answer of a sort to our original question. For having picked out, by one method or another, an event in which some person uniquely figures, or a characteristic which he alone possesses, we can say that his being the person that he is consists in his being the same person as is concerned in the event or owns the characteristic in question : the fact that we have given an account of what it is to be the same person will free the definition from circularity. It will remain contingent, a matter of good fortune, that our original point of reference does identify him ; but this we have seen to be inescapable. And if the event or characteristic which we have chosen is not sufficiently discriminating, we can always select another one instead.

Now it would seem that the best way to discover the general criteria of personal identity would be to consider what criteria are actually applied. How do we in fact succeed in recognizing people ? What makes me say, for example, that a man whom I can now see is the same man as I saw a week ago ? Perhaps only that he looks the same ; that there is, in other words, a fairly close resemblance between the appearance of this man and the appearance, as I remember it, of the man I saw

last week. This does not imply, of course, that I consciously compare them. My remembering how the man
looked last week may just consist in my recognizing
this as the same man. But I assume that my recollection would not operate in this way unless the appearances were similar. The fact that people's physical
characteristics tend to be distinctive, and that many
constant features commonly persist throughout what is
only a gradual process of change, makes this, as we
have noted, a practical method of identification. As a
criterion, it is, however, neither necessary nor sufficient.
People can look very different indeed at different
periods of their lives, and different people can look very
much alike. But suppose that I were able to trace the
movements of the man I saw a week ago from the
moment at which I saw him, and that I found that the
series of positions which he successively occupied from
that time to this terminated in the position which was
occupied by the man now before me. In that case I
should have a conclusive reason for saying that it was
the same man. This criterion of spatio-temporal continuity is not, indeed, sufficient by itself. In the
example given, it has been assumed that the man continues to look much the same ; or, if speaking of *the*
man be thought to beg the question of identity, that
each of the series of positions is occupied by a body of
roughly similar appearance. If these appearances had
changed at any point to a very considerable extent, I
might be entitled to conclude that it was not the same
man ; one must allow for the possibility that a man,
like any other object, alters his identity, that he is, as
it were, replaced by something else. Men die, and
their death does not at once destroy the identity of
their bodies ; but after a certain time at least, one

ceases to identify the man with whatever remains of his corpse, even though the criterion of spatio-temporal continuity is still fulfilled. But when it is reinforced by other factors, such as the persistence of the appropriate physical characteristics, then I think that this criterion is sufficient.

The first thing to be noticed about it is that it applies equally to persons and to things : the proof that this is the same carpet as I saw in this room a week ago follows the same lines as the proof that this is the same man. In this sense, the identity of a person is founded on the identity of his body. But is this the only sense in which we can significantly speak of a person's remaining the same, that is, of his being the same individual ? Many philosophers would say that it was. They would maintain that, whatever might be said about the union or dissociation of personalities, it was contradictory, or meaningless, to speak of a person's inhabiting different bodies at the same or different times, or of there being more than one person in the same body, or of the separation of persons from their bodies, their survival in a disembodied state. The procedure of deriving the identity of persons from the identity of their bodies is, in their view, the only one that can be significantly applied ; so long, at least, as we are using words in any ordinary sense.

If this view were shown to be correct, we should have, among other things, to re-examine the question of phenomenalism. For, as we have seen, the phenomenalist is bound to hold that the identity of any physical body is subject to analysis in terms of sense-data. Roughly speaking, it would turn on the possibility of there being a series of successive sense-fields in which corresponding positions were occupied by

P

similar sense-data : one might hope in this way to reformulate the essential condition of spatio-temporal
continuity. But so far we have allowed ourselves to
talk of sense-data only as a means of expressing how
things seem to people. And if sense-data have to be
defined in terms of persons, and the identity of persons
is itself derived from the identity of their bodies, then
the analysis of physical identity in terms of relations
between sense-data would appear to create a vicious
circle. Failing a wholly different account of personal
identity, the only way of escape would be to deny that
sense-data have to be defined in terms of persons. Thus
it might be argued that, even if one finds it necessary to
refer to persons in order to explain what is meant by a
sense-datum, there is no need to bring them into its
definition. It would, indeed, be a mistake, at least for
a phenomenalist, to offer any definition of sense-data
at all. The concept of a sense-datum is taken by him
as basic ; everything else, including the concept of a
person, is to be analysed in terms of it : and it is therefore not to be expected that it should itself be analysable
in terms of anything else. But even if the concept of a
sense-datum need not be defined, it must at least be
shown to be intelligible : and while there may, as we
have seen, be a use for it in the analysis of perception,
it is not at all clear that it remains intelligible when
its customary attachments are removed. For example,
if the existence of a given person is made to depend
upon certain relations obtaining between sense-data,
these relations must presumably be factual. That is to
say, it must be a contingent and not a necessary fact
that the sense-data in question are related to each other
in the appropriate ways. It is conceivable that they
should not have been. But this suggests that it is at

any rate logically possible for there to be sense-data
which are, so to speak, personally independent. The
relations which they have to other sense-data would
not be such as would be required to constitute a
person, or any other living thing : just as, in the case
of a hallucination, there may be sense-data which are
not the appearances of any physical object, so, on this
view of their nature, there may be actual sense-data
which do not enter into the experience of any sentient
being. It is obvious that if there were sense-data of
this kind, nobody would in fact know of their existence.
It is, at best, a logical possibility ; but is it even that ?
I confess that I am very doubtful whether this conception of unowned sense-data has any significance at all.

The same difficulty arises if, as an alternative or
supplement to the criterion of bodily identity, one tries
to make 'being the same person' consist in a relation
between experiences. This is the Humean view that
the self is 'a bundle of perceptions' ; [1] many empiricists
have held it, in one form or another. But whatever
the relations between experiences may be that are taken
to constitute self-identity — and we shall see that they
are hard to discover — they must again be factual.
Each experience is, on this view, a distinct occurrence ;
there can therefore be no logical connection between
them ; the existence of any one of them is not deducible
from the existence of any other. But this suggests that
it is logically conceivable that there should be experiences which were not the experiences of any person ;
experiences which were not owned by anything at all.
For their having an owner would depend upon their
being related in a certain way to other experiences ;
and they might in fact not be so related. This notion

___

[1] *A Treatise of Human Nature*, Book I, section vi.

of an unowned experience is not, indeed, wholly unfamiliar to philosophers : but that is not to say that it
is meaningful.

But if there cannot be experiences without someone
to have them, then it would seem that any attempt to
analyse personal identity in terms of relations between
experiences must again involve us in a vicious circle.
And since recourse to the idea of a spiritual substance
does not provide an answer, we would appear to have
no alternative but to make people's identities depend
upon the identity of their bodies, at the same time
forgoing any attempt to analyse bodily identity in terms
of sense-data. But the consequences of this position
are not very easy to accept. I agree, for example, that,
in view of the dependence of conscious processes upon
the condition of one's body, there are very good reasons
for supposing that people do not survive their death.
But this is not to say that the notion of survival is self-
contradictory, or meaningless. On the contrary, unless
the hypothesis at least made sense, one would not be
entitled to say that it was highly improbable ; for only
what is possible can be false. But if a person's identity
depends upon the identity of his body, it must be
logically impossible that he should exist in a disembodied state. If the hypothesis of survival can be
entertained at all, it must be taken as implying the
re-animation of the body. It is for this reason, perhaps,
that in some forms of religion it is orthodox to believe
in a physical resurrection. But what is sometimes overlooked is that this would require the preservation of
spatio-temporal continuity. Otherwise, it would not
be the same body. On this view, the dissolution of the
body destroys the person, no matter what subsequently
happens.

Even so, many people do believe, or say that they believe, in the existence of disembodied spirits : and, however little chance such beliefs may have of being true, it is at least not obvious that they are meaningless. Could one not imagine circumstances in which there would be reason to say that one existed without a body? Suppose, for example, that, after a period of unconsciousness, one awoke to find things appearing much as they did before, except only that one's body seemed to have vanished from the scene. One would not perceive it in any way at all, and other people, whom one would still be able to observe, although one could not make one's presence known to them, would show by their behaviour that they did not perceive it either : one would observe that they acted as if one were dead. Would it not be reasonable in such a case to conclude that one had somehow survived one's death? Such a story is indeed a fantasy. That one should continue to see and hear without sense-organs is causally impossible. But, as a fantasy, it seems to be intelligible. And, if it is even intelligible, we must be able to form a concept of personal identity which does not depend for its application upon the identity of one's body.

But, granting that there could be such a concept, by what criteria would its use be governed ? How, in our fanciful example, would it be determined that one was still the same person ? The only answer that there seems any hope in offering is that it would be necessary that one should remember the experiences that one had had before one's death. In the same way, the only means by which it seems possible to give any sense to such a hypothesis as that of reincarnation is to make it imply some continuity of memory. Suppose, for

example, that someone now living claimed to be Julius
Caesar. Our first reaction, of course, would be to dismiss him as a lunatic. Even if his character and
abilities were similar to those that historians attribute
to Caesar, we should not be in the least inclined to allow
that he really could be Caesar. But suppose that he
claimed to remember Caesar's experiences, and that
not only did his description of them agree with all the
known facts, but new discoveries were made which
confirmed his account of events in Caesar's life that
were hitherto unknown to us. In that case we should
hardly know what to say. Since the circumstances do
not in fact arise, our language is not adapted to meet
them. But if they did frequently arise, we should have
to come to a decision. We might still refuse to allow
the possibility of the same person's inhabiting more
than one body, or of his leading a series of lives with
intervals of time between them, and in that case we
should have to find another way of accounting for the
facts. As has already been remarked, we might decide
to make it possible to remember experiences that one
had never had. But we might instead prefer to say,
in such a case as I have described, that the man really
was Julius Caesar after all. This would not, indeed, be
an explanation of the facts, in any scientific sense, but
simply a redescription of them. The man's *really*
being Julius Caesar would just consist in his having
these powers of memory, and perhaps also in his
behaving in certain other ways that we chose to consider relevant. It would be a matter of fact that he
satisfied the criteria which we had laid down : but,
given that he satisfied them, to go on to ask whether he
really was the person that he claimed to be would not
be to raise a question of fact. It would be, at this stage,

a demand for a ruling. We should have simply to decide whether we thought it useful so to extend the usage of 'being the same person' that it covered cases of this sort.

This question of the possibility of reincarnation is comparatively straightforward. It is assumed that we are confronted with someone who satisfies the ordinary physical criteria of personal identity, and our problem is then only to consider whether we shall allow the continuity of memory to make him the same person as one who, if we went by the physical criteria alone, would be reckoned to be someone else. But when it comes to the possibility of a person's continuing to exist in a disembodied state, a much greater difficulty arises. For here we have to find a criterion not only for our subject's being the same person as one who is physically identified, but for his being a person at all. We have to make sense of saying that someone exists without a body, before we can raise the question whether he is the same person as one who existed with a body. And for this, continuity of memory, though it may be necessary, will not be sufficient. Assuming for the moment that it is meaningful to speak of a series of experiences, without the implication that they are the experiences of any person, we may try to thread them together by supposing that later experiences consist partly in recollections of their predecessors. If we want to enlist every member of the series, we shall have to assume that each of them is related to at least one of the others either actively or passively with respect to memory. For if memory is to be the only link between them, an experience which contained no recollection of any previous member of the series, and was not itself recollected at any later stage in it, would fall outside the series altogether. On the face of it, it would seem possible for people to have such experiences; but this possibility is removed when personal identity is made to depend solely upon memory. Furthermore, unless we assume that every detail of every experience is subsequently recollected, there will be elements that make their way into the series only because they are accompanied by memories, or by other elements which are remembered. But what is this relation of accompanying? We may say that it is the relation that holds between two items of experience if and only if they are parts of the same total experience at any given moment. But what is meant here by a total experience is just the experience of one and the same person. We can hold that the relation between its parts is *sui generis*, but then we can also hold that the relation between the successive experiences of the same person is *sui generis*: and in that case we do not need to bring in memory at all.

A further objection is that to remember an experience entails claiming it as an experience of one's own: from which it would seem to follow that personal identity cannot be founded on this type of memory since it is already presupposed by it. But here the circle may be only apparent. To claim an experience as one's own may consist in nothing more than a disposition to use first person language in describing it. It may, indeed, be argued that the use of first person language itself presupposes the notion of personal identity, but I am not sure that this is so. I think that one can, for example, come to use the word 'I' correctly and intelligently, without necessarily thinking of the series of one's own experiences as being in any way related; it seems to me possible even that the use of the word

should be learned by someone who was not self-
conscious at all. And this is borne out by the fact that
to ask ' Is this experience mine ? ' is not to raise a serious
question. Neither is this just a peculiarity of the em-
ployment of the present tense. It is rather that to refer
to an experience demonstratively is to preclude any
doubt about its ownership ; there can be no question
whose it is. The inference which I wish to draw
from this is that in using the first person, one need not
be raising the question whether any criteria of personal
identity are satisfied ; otherwise, it would always be
sensible to ask of any experience whether it was one's
own. Admittedly, the experience in question will not
in fact be one's own, unless the criteria are satisfied :
but I suggest that it does not follow that one need
actually be stating that they are satisfied when one
claims an experience by the use of first person language.
I conclude, therefore, with some hesitation, that if the
other obstacles to founding personal identity upon
memory were overcome, this charge of circularity could
be met.

This is, however, only a subsidiary question. The
major objection on the score of circularity still remains.
I find myself here in the sort of dilemma that frequently
arises in philosophy. On the one hand, I am inclined
to hold that personal identity can be constituted by the
presence of a certain factual relation between experiences. On the other hand, I doubt if it is meaningful
to talk of experiences except as the experiences of a
person ; or at least of an animate creature of some kind.
As I have already remarked, these views appear to be
inconsistent with each other, but I think it possible
that they can be reconciled. In saying that the relations
between experiences which are supposed to constitute

personal identity are factual, I am implying that it is never necessary that any two experiences should be related by them. Either one of the experiences in question might occur, even if the other did not. But while it follows from this that there are no experiences in particular to which any given experience need be so related, it does not follow that it could fail to stand in any such relation to any experiences at all. It does not follow that the experience could exist entirely on its own. And indeed the suggestion that there are experiences which so exist is one that I do find nonsensical; there would seem to be no conceivable way in which its truth or falsehood could be tested. But if it is nonsensical, we cannot talk of experiences without implying that they have owners. And then we seem to involve ourselves in a circle when we make the existence of persons consist only in a certain relationship between experiences. But I do not think that this circle is vicious. It shows that we could not understand what is meant by an experience unless we already understood what was meant by being a person; but, as we have already seen in other instances, to understand what is meant by an expression does not entail that one can give a satisfactory analysis of its use. So even if the existence of an experience entails the existence of a person, an analysis of personal identity in terms of experiences could still be informative. What is disturbing is the implication that the relations between experiences, which would furnish such an analysis, must be logically necessary. But they will be necessary only in the sense that from the fact that an experience occurs it will follow, on this view, that there are some other experiences to which it bears the relations in question. But the other experiences are not specified.

Any statement to the effect that two given experiences are so related will remain contingent. Thus, of the two principles which Hume admitted that he could neither renounce nor reconcile — 'that all our distinct perceptions are distinct existences' and 'that the mind never perceives any real connection among distinct existences' [1]— we must, I think, renounce or at least reinterpret the first. Distinct perceptions are distinct existences inasmuch as, given any set of perceptions, A, B, C, . . . , the existence of any one of them is compatible with the non-existence of any of the others. But if it does not make sense to talk of perceptions without a percipient, then, on the Humean view that the self is 'a bundle of perceptions', the existence of any one perception A must entail the existence of some other. It is consistent with the existence of A that B, C . . . should not have existed, but it is implied that if they had not existed some other perceptions would have taken their place. And the same applies to sense-data, which are indeed to be counted as perceptions, in Hume's sense. Their existence may be made to depend upon the existence of physical objects, or of other sense-data, but no sense-datum can exist entirely on its own. We have seen, however, that this alone does not exclude the possibility of giving a phenomenalist account of the self.

None of this proves, of course, that there are any other criteria of personal identity than those that depend upon the identity of the body. We have not succeeded in discovering any relation by which the constituents of Hume's bundles could be adequately held together. Some continuity of memory is necessary, but not, I think, sufficient. It needs to be backed by

[1] *Treatise of Human Nature*, Appendix.

some other relation of which, perhaps, nothing more illuminating can be said than that it is the relation that holds between experiences when they are constituents of the same consciousness. The alternative is to regard it as a necessary proposition that a person's existence is tied to the existence of his body. But I am not convinced that this proposition is necessary, though I believe that it is true.

(iii)
The privacy of experience

Whether or not it is possible to conceive of minds existing apart from bodies, it is the view of common sense that they are at least distinguishable. Even if we cannot allow ourselves to speak of minds as substances, we are able to contrast mental with physical objects or events. And one of the characteristics which are ascribed to mental objects or events is that they are in some way private. Thus it is commonly held that our thoughts and feelings, our dreams and imaginings, our sensations and memories, are things to which we alone have access. We can communicate them to others, in the sense that we are able to convey information about them, but we cannot transfer them to others. It is true that one does quite frequently speak of different persons sharing the same thoughts or feelings, but it would generally be held that what is meant by this is that these thoughts or feelings are similar, or proceed from similar causes, not that they are literally the same. On the other hand, it is commonly assumed that different people do perceive the same physical objects. In this way, a distinction comes to be drawn, among our experiences, between those that are directed 'out-

wards' towards a public world and those that dwell
only on the private stage of one's own consciousness.
But these 'outer' experiences are themselves turned
'inwards' by the introduction of sense-data. It is maintained, as we have seen, that two different persons
perceiving the same physical object is 'really' a matter
of each one's sensing his own sense-data; and these
sense-data, though they may be similar, cannot be the
same. And so we reach the philosophical contention
that all one's experiences are private to oneself.

But how is this proposition to be proved? It does
not seem to follow from any of the competing theories
of personal identity. I do not see how anyone who
believed that the self was a substance could deduce
from this that it was impossible for two different selves
to own the same experience. If personal identity is
made to depend upon the identity of the body, it does
follow that two different people cannot 'occupy' the
same body, but this does not by itself entail that they
can have no experiences in common. It would have
to be shown that all one's experiences were in some
way located in one's body, and it is not evident that this
must be so, even on the assumption that one can always
give a sense to saying that they have any location at all.
And if a person can be constituted by a suitably related
series of experiences, why should not two such series
interlock? Why should not different 'bundles of perceptions' contain at least one common element?

The answer is that there is a reason only if one
chooses to find one. The question whether an object
is public or private is fundamentally a question of
language; it depends upon the conventions which
we follow in making judgements of identity. Thus
physical objects are public because it makes sense to

say of different people that they are perceiving the same physical object ; mental images are private because it does not make sense to say of different people that they are having the same mental image ; they can be imagining the same thing, but it is impossible that their respective mental images should be literally the same. But these conventions could be altered. Just as one may be able to break down the perception by different people of the same physical object into the sensing of private sense-data, so one could publicize the experiences which existing usage insists on keeping private. It would simply be a matter of formulating the conditions which would have to be satisfied for different people to share the same experience. It is not even difficult to imagine that we should have empirical motives for acting in this way. Suppose, for example, that people's feelings were very much more uniform than they actually are, so that whenever anyone felt bored, or happy, or angry, or depressed, his neighbours nearly always felt the same. In that case, we might very well find a use for saying that there was not a multiplicity of feelings, one to each person, but a single feeling, one and the same for all, which different people experienced in different ways. Certain people might fail to experience it at all, just as certain people fail to perceive physical objects which are in their neighbourhood. There might be illusions of feeling, corresponding to illusions of perception. But the feeling would still be there, just as the physical object is there whatever illusion someone may be having. To make the analogy with physical objects closer still, one might make it possible for feelings to exist when no one was actually feeling them. This might be said in cases where the normal conditions in which the feeling

habitually occurred were present, but some special
factor, such as the drugging or hypnotizing of the person
in question, intervened. To argue, then, that the feeling could not *really* exist if no one felt it would be
to protest against this usage. It would correspond to
the protest against our actual use of language which is
made by those who argue that physical objects cannot
exist unless they are perceived.

The point of this fantasy is to show how the distinction between what is public and what is private
depends upon a contingent matter of fact. We do not
find it useful to publicize feelings, or sensations, or
thoughts, or images, because they vary so much from
person to person : we do find it useful to publicize
physical objects because of the extent to which the
perceptions of different people agree. But it is not
difficult to imagine that the two should be on a level,
or even that the position should be reversed. This is
not to say, however, that the distinction, as we have it,
is itself empirical. When philosophers assert that experiences are private, they are referring to a necessary
truth. It would be a contradiction to speak of the
feelings of two different people as being numerically
identical : it is logically impossible that one person
should literally feel another's pain. But these points
of logic are based upon linguistic usages which have,
as it were, the empirical facts in view. If the facts
were different, the usage might be changed. There
might still be experiences that were not actually shared ;
but it would not be decided logically that they were
unshareable.

Nevertheless, even if this were to happen, the possibility of making all experiences private would still
remain. Even if our language were such that we

attached no sense to talking of individual experiences, allowing only the existence of common experiences in which different people could participate, it would still be open to philosophers to argue that when different people were said to have the same experience, what should be said was that each of them was having his own. This would be paradoxical, just as it is now paradoxical for philosophers to argue that when different people are said to perceive the same physical object, what should be said is that each of them perceives his own sense-data. But, as a revision of usage, it would be legitimate. Moreover, these philosophers could claim that there was a sense in which their notation brought them closer to the facts. For they would be able to maintain with reason that the existence of a common experience depended upon the existence, or at the very least upon the possibility, of individual experiences : whereas the converse would not necessarily hold.

But, this being so, a philosophical problem is created. If we allow this way of speaking, and I do not see how we can be entitled to exclude it, then the claim that one is perceiving a public object, whatever may be its nature, will always be founded on the fact that one is having a private experience. The existence of the public object will be established by the fact that other people are also having, or at least disposed to have, the appropriate experiences. But how is one ever to discover that this is so ? What justification can I have for believing even that there are any experiences other than my own ?

Well, why should I not observe them ? We are taking it as a necessary fact that one person cannot have the experiences of another. It is not allowed to be even logically possible that I should think my neighbour's thoughts, or dream his dreams, or enjoy his memories, or feel his pains. But does it follow from this that I cannot inspect his thoughts or sensations or feelings ? They are private to him in the sense that only he has them, but does this mean that he cannot display them to anyone else ? We do, indeed, talk of people displaying their thoughts and feelings, but this is ordinarily understood to mean that they are exhibiting signs of them. Is it impossible that they should exhibit the experiences themselves ? Suppose that the occurrence of telepathy were well authenticated. Would not this be a case of one person's directly inspecting the private experiences of another ? Neither need we have recourse to anything so out of the way as telepathy. We quite often come to know what people are thinking or feeling simply by observing them. One looks at a man and sees that he is angry or perplexed or bored or amused. Why should this not be construed as a direct observation not only of his outward behaviour but of his inner state ?

The answer is that we can so construe it, if it pleases us. We can give a sense to saying that one person inspects or 'directly observes' the private experiences of another. He may be said to do so just in those cases where he knows what experiences the other person is having, and does not come to know it through any process of inference. In the ordinary case one is inclined to say that there is at least an unconscious process of inference ; a person's feelings are read off from his looks. Though we do not consciously proceed from one to the other, we should not know what he was feeling unless he displayed some characteristic signs. But it is conceivable that one should come to

Q

know what another person was thinking or feeling even though he displayed none of the appropriate signs. It would simply be that one was confident that he was in the state in question, and that one was so often right as to be justified in claiming the title to be sure. For this to happen it might be necessary that one should be in the other person's presence ; or it might be that one could do it even in his absence. I believe that it is mostly this second case that is envisaged when people discuss the possibility of telepathy. And certainly we have no reason to deny *a priori* that such things could occur.

But even if we decide to give this meaning to 'directly observing the experiences of another', our difficulty is not removed. It reappears when we are asked to justify in any particular instance the claim that the performance which we so describe has really taken place. For even a telepathic experience, it will be argued, is private to oneself ; the peculiarity which is attributed to it is that of revealing what is going on in someone else's mind ; but this does not make it any the less an experience of one's own, and considered merely as an experience of one's own it is logically in- dependent of the experiences of anybody else, even of that which it purports to reveal. There would be no contradiction in allowing that it existed even though the other person's experience did not. In that case it would not, indeed, be telepathic, if its being telepathic is taken to imply that it yields knowledge of the other person's mental state. But then in saying that it is telepathic we shall not be merely describing the character of the experience : we shall also be implying that the belief to which it gives rise, concerning the other person's mental state, is true. And this claim needs to be justified. But then it is just the question how such claims are ever to be justified that constitutes our problem. Here again the naïve realist's solution of the problem amounts to a dismissal of it. He insists that we do know what we think we know, but he does not explain how it is possible that we should know it.

(iv)
What can we communicate?

Now the obvious answer to the question how we know about the experiences of others is that they are communicated to us, either through their natural manifestations in the form of gestures, tears, laughter, play of feature and so forth, or by the use of language. A very good way to find out what another person is thinking or feeling is to ask him. He may not answer, or if he does answer he may not answer truly, but very often he will. The fact that the information which people give about themselves can be deceptive does not entail that it is never to be trusted. We do not depend on it alone: it may be, indeed, that the inferences which we draw from people's non-verbal behaviour are more secure than those that we base upon what they say about themselves, that actions speak more honestly than words. But were it not that we can rely a great deal upon words, we should know very much less about each other than we do.

At this point, however, a difficulty arises. If I am to acquire information in this way about another person's experiences, I must understand what he says about them. And this would seem to imply that I attach the same meaning to his words as he does. But how, it may be asked, can I ever be sure that this is so ? He tells me that he is in pain, but may it not be that what he understands by pain is something quite different from anything that I should call by that name ? He tells me that something looks red to him, but how do I know that what he calls 'red' is not what I should call 'blue', or that it is not a colour unlike any that I have ever seen, or that it does not differ from anything that I should even take to be a colour ? All these things would seem to be possible. Yet how are such questions ever to be decided ?

In face of this difficulty, some philosophers have maintained that experiences as such are incommunicable.[1] They have held that in so far as one uses words to refer to the content of one's experiences, they can be intelligible only to oneself. No one else can understand them, because no one else can get into one's mind to verify the statements which they express. What can be communicated, on this view, is structure. I have no means of knowing that other people have sensations or feelings which are in any way like my own. I cannot tell even that they mean the same by the words which they use to refer to physical objects, since the perceptions which they take as establishing the existence of these objects may be utterly different from any that I have ever had myself. If I could get into my neighbour's head to see what it is that he refers to as a table, I might fail to recognize it altogether, just as I might fail to recognize anything that he is disposed to call a colour or a pain. On the other hand, however different the content of his experience may be from

---

[1] This view was current, at one time, in the Vienna Circle. Cf. M. Schlick, *Allgemeine Erkenntnislehre*, and R. Carnap, *Der logische Aufbau der Welt*.

mine, I do know that its structure is the same. The
proof that it is the same is that his use of words agrees
with mine, in so far as he applies them in a corresponding way. However different the table that he perceives
may be from the table that I perceive, he agrees with
me in saying of certain things that they are tables and
of others that they are not. No matter what he actually
sees when he refers to colour, his classification of
things according to their colour is the same as mine.
Even if his conception of pain is quite different from
my own, his behaviour when he says that he is in pain
is such as I consider to be appropriate. Thus the
possible differences of content can, and indeed must be
disregarded. What we can establish is that our experiences are similarly ordered. It is this similarity of
structure that provides us with our common world :
and it is only descriptions of this common world,
that is, descriptions of structure, that we are able to
communicate.

On this view, the language which different people
seem to share consists, as it were, of flesh and bones.
The bones represent its public aspect ; they serve alike
for all. But each of us puts flesh upon them in accordance with the character of his experiences. Whether
one person's way of clothing the skeleton is or is not
the same as another's is an unanswerable question. The
only thing that we can be satisfied about is the identity
of the bones.

This theory has, I think, a certain plausibility. Its
weakness appears when one tries to make it more
precise. For what exactly is this distinction between
structure and content supposed to be ? Can one find
any examples of a statement which is purely about
structure, a statement which belongs entirely to the

public part of language ? Descriptions of spatial relationships, perhaps, where the terms between which the
relations hold are left qualitatively unidentified ? But
what anyone understands by such words as 'above' or
'beyond' or 'to the left of' depends no less upon the
character of his experience than what he understands
by 'sweet' or 'blue'. Even the understanding of so
bare a statement as that two things are similar in some
respect requires that similarity be identifiable in one's
experience. If I cannot know that another person
means the same as I do by 'table' I cannot know that
he means the same by 'similarity'. Even the use of
numerals, in the expression of statements which are
not wholly formal, cannot be understood unless one
can interpret the results of counting or measuring
operations. And how can I be sure that my neighbour's interpretation is the same as mine ? How can I
be sure that if I were to perceive what he counts as a
group of four things I should not reckon them to be
four hundred ? I am not saying, indeed, that I have
any serious reason for entertaining doubts on such a
point ; but only that if there are reasons for doubt they
apply to any descriptive use of language, to the attribution of relations as much as to the attribution of
qualities, to statements about structure no less than to
statements about content.

But what of the argument that other people's
behaviour, while revealing nothing of the content of
their experience, does at least show me that its structure is the same as that of mine ? It is suggested that
even if I cannot know that someone else means the
same as I do by the words he uses, I do know that he
applies them to the same things. But if I can know
nothing whatsoever about the content of his experience,

then I cannot know even that he does apply his words
in a way that is formally consistent with my own. For
all that I can tell, what sounds to me like a repetition
of the same word does not sound so to him, what looks
to me like an object of the same type as those to which
the word was previously applied does not look so to
him. The fact that he behaves as if we understood
each other, that he responds in the appropriate way to
my statements or requests, may prove that our respective
worlds are somehow geared together, but it does not
prove that their structure is the same. Once more, I
am not maintaining that different people do not understand each other, or that this is not proved by their
behaviour. I am maintaining only that there is no
warrant here for separating structure and content, for
arguing that structure can be communicated whereas
content cannot. Indeed, this whole attempt to draw a
distinction within descriptive language between what
can and cannot be communicated appears to me misguided. If there were something that my neighbour
could not communicate to me, I should be left in
ignorance of his meaning : I should not know what he
was talking about. But if I am in a position to say
what it is that he has failed to communicate to me, he
has in fact succeeded. To say, for example, that he
cannot tell me that he is in pain implies that I understand what is meant by his being in pain : for otherwise I should attach no meaning to saying that *this*
was what he could not tell me. But if I understand
what is meant by his being in pain, there is no reason
in logic why he should not be able to tell me that he is
in pain. And the same applies to any other statement
that he may choose to make about the content of his
experience. What the analysis of these statements is,

whether, for example, they have a different meaning for him from the meaning that they have for me, is another question. We shall return to it later on.

(v)
The thesis of physicalism

This mistake of supposing that only structure is communicable arises from a combination of errors. The philosophers who made it assumed that for a language to be public it must be used to refer to public objects. But they also believed that to make an empirical statement was ultimately to refer to one's own experiences. And since they held that all one's experiences were private to oneself, they seemed bound to conclude that an empirical statement could never be public ; that it could be intelligible only to the person who made it. But finding this result too paradoxical, they sought to mitigate the privacy of experiences by assigning them a common structure. And so they came to hold that structure, being the only common object, was the only thing communicable. But in the first place it is false that for a language to be public it must refer to public objects. What makes a language public is that one person's use of it is intelligible to another : and, as I hope to show presently, from the fact that one cannot literally share the experiences of another person it does not follow that one cannot understand what he says about them. And, secondly, it is also false that in making an empirical statement one is always referring to one's own experiences. Empirical statements may be said to refer to experiences, in the sense that it is only through the occurrence of some experience that they can be shown to be true or false, but it need not be one's own experience ; it need not be the experience of any given person. To put it another way, in the case where an empirical statement does not itself record an actual or possible experience, it may be required that some such 'experiential' statement be derivable from it : but this experiential statement may be impersonal. If it is true, it will in fact be because someone has the experience in question. But its truth need not depend upon the identity of the person who has the experience. Some other person might have done as well.

The same errors have been responsible for what is known as the thesis of physicalism ; the thesis that when one appears to be speaking about minds one is really always speaking about bodies ; or, to put it more precisely, that to say anything about a person's thoughts or feelings, or sensations, or private experiences of any kind, is always equivalent to saying something about his physical condition, or behaviour, where this applies to the statements that one makes about oneself as well as to those that one makes about other people. For the ground on which this thesis is maintained is that it is only if such statements are interpreted 'physicalistically' that they can convey any information from one person to another. Otherwise, not only should we not be able to communicate our experiences ; we should not, so it is argued, even be able to exchange any information about physical objects. Thus Carnap, who uses the expression 'physical language' to designate the class of statements which ostensibly refer to physical objects or occurrences, and the expression 'protocol language' to designate the class of statements which ostensibly refer to a person's private experiences, maintains that our understanding of the physical language requires that the protocol language be included in it. He holds that 'physical statements' must entail 'protocol statements' in order to be verifiable. Were this not so, 'physical statements would float in a void disconnected, in principle, from all experience'. But if protocol statements are deducible from physical statements they must, he thinks, themselves refer to physical facts. For the only alternative is that physical statements refer to the contents of experience; and Carnap argues that this is excluded by the fact that experiences are private. If S_1 and S_2 are different people, 'S_1's protocol language refers to the content of S_1's experience, S_2's protocol language to the content of S_2's experience. What can the intersubjective physical language refer to? It must refer to the content of the experiences of both S_1 and S_2. This is however impossible for the realms of experience of two persons do not overlap.' He therefore concludes that 'there is no solution free from contradictions in this direction'.[1]

Once more it is assumed that if experiences are private they are describable only in a private language; and from this it is inferred that if protocol statements were interpreted purely as records of experience, the fact that they were entailed by physical statements would mean that the public language, which we use to refer to physical objects, would dissolve into a set of private languages, having nothing in common with each other. But this conclusion does not hold. The statements of what Carnap calls the physical language may be said to refer to experiences, in the sense that they are verified by them. But in that case, as we have already remarked, they refer to them neutrally. Let

[1] R. Carnap, *The Unity of Science*, p. 82.

us suppose, for example, that S_1 verifies a physical statement p by having an experience e_1 and that S_2 verifies p by having an experience e_2. So long as e_1 and e_2 are both of the appropriate type, they respectively justify S_1 and S_2 in accepting p; and the fact that they are not identical with one another does not lead to any contradiction at all. Thus, the answer to Carnap's question 'What can the intersubjective physical language refer to?' is that it refers, in this sense, neither to the 'private world' of S_1 nor to that of S_2, but to the experiences of anyone you please.

It does not follow from this that the thesis of physicalism is false. Independently of this fallacious argument, it might still be the case that every assertion of what would appear to be a mental fact is logically equivalent to the assertion of some physical fact. But when it is considered on its own merits, this thesis does not appear at all convincing. Certainly, in one's own case, it seems necessary to distinguish the sensations, or images, or feelings that one has from the physical states or actions by which they are manifested. However intimate the relation may be between an 'inner' experience and its 'outward' expression, it is not necessary that the one should accompany the other. I can behave as if I had thoughts, or sensations, or feelings that I in fact do not have; and I can have thoughts or feelings that I keep entirely to myself. No doubt I could always express them if I chose; perhaps I am always disposed to express them; but this is not to say that my having them consists in nothing more than my being disposed to perform certain actions, or utter certain words. Again, it may be argued that every so-called mental event has its physiological counterpart, that each of one's experiences is, as it were, recorded on one's brain. This is a physiological hypothesis which has yet to be adequately verified, but it may very well be true. Even so, it would not follow that the experience was identical with its physical correlate, that to describe one's sensations or feelings was logically equivalent to describing the condition of one's brain. For the existence of this psycho-physical parallelism, if it does exist, is a scientific *discovery*. The connection between the mental and the physical events has to be established by experiment. But this implies that they are not identical. For if they were identical, experiments would not be needed. The connection could be established by logic alone.

The question whether one can have experiences which find no 'external' expression is complicated by the fact that a number of the words which seem to stand for mental events or processes are actually used in such a way that they include a reference to physical behaviour. Thus to be angry, or jealous, or bored, or gay, or happy is not merely, or even primarily, to have a special feeling; it is also to display certain physical signs, to behave, or be disposed to behave, in the appropriate fashion. If I go only by introspection I may mistake my mood; other people who note only my demeanour may judge the state of my feelings better than I do myself. But from the fact that we speak of feelings in a wider as well as in a narrower sense, the fact that what might pass for a description of one's feeling is commonly taken to imply rather more than the existence of the feeling as something privately and immediately felt, it does not follow that these feelings, in the narrow 'mental' sense, do not exist at all : nor does it follow that they cannot be described.

And when it comes to other mental phenomena, such as sensations or images, the connection with physical events seems wholly synthetic; the descriptions which we give of them would not ordinarily be construed as entailing any reference to what is publicly observable.

Finally, the argument which Carnap brings in favour of physicalism, that otherwise 'physical statements would float in a void disconnected, in principle, from all experience', actually works the other way. For the whole point of 'protocol statements' was that they characterized experiences. It was this that gave them their privileged position. But if they themselves are to be construed as statements about the condition of one's body, they will no longer play this special rôle. Like other physical statements, they will have to be empirically verifiable: but their translation into the class of physical statements will leave us without any means of describing the experiences by which they or their fellows are to be verified. The place that they were designed to occupy in language could indeed be left vacant; one may know what experiences are required to verify a given physical statement, without in fact having the resources for describing them: but it must be possible that such descriptions should be found.

(vi)

The analysis and justification of statements about other minds

To apply the physicalist thesis to one's own experiences is, as it were, to pretend to be anaesthetized. But this does not hold for the experiences of others, if one cannot be aware of them in the way that one is

244   THE PROBLEM OF KNOWLEDGE

aware of one's own. It is, therefore, maintained by some philosophers that there is a radical difference in the analysis of 'mental' facts, according as they relate to other people or to oneself. The suggestion is that if I say of myself that I am in pain I am referring to a feeling of which I alone am conscious ; if my statement is true it may be that I also show certain outward signs of pain, but I do not imply that this is so : it is not part of what my statement means. Or even granting that it is part of what my statement means, it is not all that it means. But if I say of someone else that he is in pain, all that my statement is supposed to mean is that he displays signs of pain, that his body is in such and such a state, or that he behaves, or is disposed to behave, in such and such ways. For this is all that I can conceivably observe.[1]

An obvious objection to this thesis is that it entails that the statements which I make about my feelings cannot have the same meaning for any other person as they have for me. Thus, if someone asks me whether I am in pain and I answer that I am, my reply, as I understand it, is not an answer to his question. For I am reporting the occurrence of a certain feeling ; whereas, so far as he was concerned, his question could only have been a question about my physical condition. So also, if he says that my reply is false, he is not strictly contradicting me : for all that he can be denying is that I exhibited the proper signs of pain, and this is not what I asserted ; it is what he understood me to be asserting but not what I understood myself. In so far as there is a regular connection between such conscious states and the physical manifestations by which they are defined for others, this discrepancy might not be

[1] Cf. my Language, Truth and Logic, ch. 7.

practically important. But the connection is not perfect; and the fact that it might not obtain is itself sufficient for our argument.

Moreover, in the form in which it is usually held, the theory is inconsistent.[1] For a philosopher who maintains it does not merely wish to argue that the statements which he makes about his own feelings have a different meaning for him from that which they can have for anyone else. He wishes his theory to have a general application : it is supposed to be true of all of us that when we talk about our own mental states, we are referring to experiences of which we can be directly aware, but when we talk about the mental states of others we are referring to their physical condition or behaviour. But if the theory were correct, this distinction between the mental and the physical, between what is private and what is public, could not be made in any case but one's own. If I cannot distinguish between another person's feelings and their physical expression, I cannot suppose that he distinguishes them. Or rather, if I do suppose that he distinguishes them, I can be supposing only that he is guilty of a logical error, that he is taking two forms of expression to refer to different things when they in fact refer to the same. I cannot both admit the distinction that he makes and say that it has no meaning for me. The picture which this theory tries to present is that of a number of people enclosed within the fortresses of their own experiences. They can observe the battlements of other fortresses, but they cannot penetrate them. Not only that, but they cannot even conceive that anything lies behind them. All their discourse

[1] Martin Shearn, *A Study of Analytical Behaviourism*, Ph.D. thesis in the University of London.

about other fortresses, as opposed to their own, is
limited to a description of the battlements. But the
philosopher who paints this picture is, by the terms of
the theory, himself immured in such a fortress. If he
talks about the fortresses of others, he can be doing
no more than describing their battlements. Thus, if
his picture were accurate he could not paint it. He
could not even imagine that other people were in the
same situation as himself.

So long as he does not attempt to generalize his
thesis, our philosopher may indeed hold that only he
can have experiences. But since I do have experiences,
I know that this view is false if the philosopher be
any other than myself. And since I can surmise that
another philosopher holds it, I myself concede that it
is false. But this does not dispose of the problem. Let
it be granted that in the sense in which we severally
claim to have experiences we can also attribute them
to others. There is still the philosophical question
how this is possible.

The source of the difficulty, here again, is that one
is postulating the existence of something that one could
not conceivably observe. But, once more, it is necessary to distinguish between statements which are unverifiable by anyone and those that are unverifiable by
some particular person. We saw, in the case of statements about the past, that the fact that they were made
by persons who could not observe the events to which
they referred did not entail that these events were
altogether unobservable. Might not the same apply to
statements about 'other minds'? [1]

There is, however, a special difficulty in the case of

---

[1] Cf. my 'One's Knowledge of Other Minds', *Theoria*, vol. xix.
Reprinted in *Philosophical Essays*.

statements about other minds, which differentiates
them from statements about the past. It can be
argued that one's inability to observe a past event is
due to the accident of one's position in time : we have
seen that the fact that a person lives at such and such a
date is not essential to his being the person that he is.
But it is not an accident that one is not someone else.
One might indeed be a very different sort of person
from the person that one is : one might be very much
more like some other person than one is in fact. But
it is not even logically possible that one should be
identical with another person. It is possible that there
should have been only one of us and not two, that one
or other of us should not have existed ; but this is not
to say that we might have been, or that we might
become, identical. Thus, if my inability to observe
what goes on in the mind of another is due to our
being separate persons, there is no possible adjustment
of my situation by which it could be overcome.[1]

Nevertheless, there is a way in which the parallel
still holds. In the sense in which there is no special
class of statements about the past, so there is no special
class of statements about other minds. The use of
pronouns, such as 'you' or 'he', may indicate that the
person referred to is someone other than the speaker,
just as the use of tenses may indicate that the event is
earlier than the time at which the statement is made ;
but the meaning of a statement which refers to a
person's experiences is not affected by the fact that it
is made by someone other than the person himself, any
more than the meaning of a statement which refers to
an event occurring at a certain position in time is

[1] John Watling, 'Ayer on Other Minds', *Theoria*, vol. xx, nos. 1-3,
and Shearn, *op. cit.*

R

affected by the fact that it is made at a subsequent time. In either instance, the statement may be formulated in such a way as to convey information about the circumstances in which it is expressed, but this information is not part of what it states. In the case of a statement, which is in fact about 'another mind', what is stated is, in effect, that someone who answers to a certain description has such and such an experience. To understand it, one must therefore know what it would be like to answer to the description and to have the experience in question. Now, if I am not the person to whom the statement refers, it is not possible that I, being the person that I am, should answer to the description: or rather, if I could answer to it, this would prove only that the description chosen was not a sufficient identification; for if the description does sufficiently identify the person in question, it is impossible that any other person should answer to it, while continuing to answer to the descriptions which sufficiently identify himself. It does not follow, however, that I cannot conceive of myself as answering to it. Suppose, for example, that I am told of the experiences of a child, who is described in a way that, for all I know, could apply to myself. I may come to believe that I was the child in question. Later, I may discover that I was not: but I do not then cease to understand the statement about the child's experiences, nor do I attach a different meaning to it. Admittedly, if I then think of myself as someone to whom the description does not apply, I cannot also suppose that it does. I cannot consistently conceive of myself both as being a person of a certain sort and as being a person of a different sort. But I am not logically obliged to think of myself as satisfying any particular description : and so long as I do not limit the possibilities by forming a picture of myself with which anything that I imagine has to be reconciled, I can conceive of having any consistent set of characteristics that you please. All that is required is that the possession of these characteristics be something that is in itself empirically verifiable. The fact that I do not have the characteristics chosen, or even that I could not have them, being the person that I am, does not therefore entail that I cannot know what it would be like to have them. And if I can know what it would be like to satisfy a certain set of descriptions and to have a certain experience, then I can understand a statement to the effect that someone who satisfies these descriptions is having that experience, independently of the question whether that person is, or could be, myself.

But if it be allowed that one can attach a meaning to statements which refer to the experiences of others, and, what is more, the same meaning as is attached to them by those to whom the experiences are ascribed, then it becomes open to us to justify our acceptance of such statements by an inductive argument. On the basis of my own experience I form a general hypothesis to the effect that certain physical phenomena are accompanied by certain feelings. When I observe that some other person is in the appropriate physical state, I am thereby enabled to infer that he is having these feelings ; feelings which are similar to those that in similar circumstances I have myself. The objection taken by some philosophers to this argument is that its conclusion is unverifiable ; but I have tried to show that this objection can be met.

Even so, the argument does not seem very strong. The objection that one is generalizing from a single instance can perhaps be countered by maintaining that it is not a matter of extending to all other persons a conclusion which has been found to hold for only one, but rather of proceeding from the fact that certain properties have been found to be conjoined in various contexts to the conclusion that they remain conjoined in further contexts. Thus I have discovered, for example, that when I have an infected tooth I feel considerable pain and that I tend to express this feeling in certain characteristic ways. And I have found that these connections hold independently of other circumstances such as the place where I happen to be, the way in which I am dressed, the state of the weather, the nature of my political opinions, and so forth. On the other hand, I have found that it is not independent of the state of my nervous system. So when I observe that some other person is similarly afflicted and that he acts in a similar way, I may infer that a similar feeling is also present, unless there is something in the circumstances that would make the connection fail. If I knew that he had been anaesthetized, for instance, I might conclude that he did not feel pain; that, although he behaved as if he felt it, he was only pretending. But other features of the context, the colour of his hair, the date of his birth, the number of his children, and many other items among those that went to make him 'another person', I should rightly dismiss as irrelevant. So the question that I put is not: Am I justified in assuming that what I have found to be true only of myself is also true of others? but: Having found that in various circumstances the possession of certain properties is united with the possession of a certain feeling, does this union continue to obtain when the circumstances are still further varied? The basis

of the argument is broadened by absorbing the difference of persons into the difference of the situations in
which the psycho-physical connections are supposed to
hold.

This way of presenting the argument makes it
stronger, but it may still be objected that it hardly
makes it strong enough. For the variety of conditions
in which I can in fact test any of these psycho-physical
hypotheses is extremely limited. There are a great
many properties of which I cannot divest myself and a
great many that I cannot acquire ; and among them are
properties which are peculiar to me, or peculiar to some
other person. Might it not be that the possession of
one such property, say the property of having been
born at the exact time and place at which I was, is
necessary for being conscious ? Or that having just
those finger-prints that my neighbour has is a
barrier to consciousness ? These suggestions seem
absurd, but what right have I to dismiss them ? [1] My
neighbour's having the finger-prints he has does not
prevent him from behaving like anybody else. He displays every sign of consciousness when one would
expect him to. But this is not disputed. What is in
question is my right to infer the existence of something
'behind' this behaviour. I distinguish my own states
of consciousness from their physical expressions and I
wish to do the same for others. But then the possibility that they differ from me, or from one another,
just in this respect, has a claim to be considered
seriously.

Moreover, if my belief in other minds depended on
this inductive argument, its strength should be pro-
portionate both to the variety of my own experiences

[1] Shearn, *op. cit.*

and to the extent to which I had discovered physical resemblances between other people and myself. I should need to vary my own attributes as much as possible, in order to increase the range over which my psycho-physical hypotheses were known to hold, and I should have to examine other people to see how far the analogy could be made to extend. The further I could extend it, the more confident I should be in ascribing consciousness to them. But in fact it does not seem that I need make any such experiments in order to discover that other people are conscious.[1] Their consciousness is expressed in their demeanour; in their manner of acting, in their use of language. If I discovered that someone who exhibited these signs of consciousness was physiologically very different from myself, that he had, for example, a different type of nervous system, I should not conclude that the signs were fallacious, that he was not conscious after all. I should conclude rather that I had been mistaken in supposing that in order to be conscious it was necessary to have a nervous system like my own.

This is not to say that the resemblances which I observe between myself and others do not supply the foundation for my belief in the existence and character of their experiences. If I did not know that I had thoughts and feelings and sensations and that I revealed them in characteristic ways, I should have no basis at all for ascribing them to others. Neither in saying that the fact that people are conscious comes out in their demeanour do I wish to imply that the two are to be identified. It is rather that their displays of thought and feeling afford the best evidence that I can have for the existence of what they are said to manifest.

[1] Cf. Watling, *op. cit.*

Consideration of the physiological resemblances between myself and others plays a secondary rôle.

But still the sceptic can maintain that if this is the
best evidence, he has no reason to be convinced : it
does not even measure up to the standards of scientific
proof. And in a way he is right. He is right on the
subject of other minds just as he is right on the subject
of the past. If it is required of an inductive argument
that the generalization to which it leads should be
based on a wide variety of experienced instances, both
candidates fail the test. One has only a limited experience of the connection of 'inner' states with their outer
manifestations ; and one has no experience at all of
the connection of a present with a past event. But
these are not ordinary limitations ; what is suspect
about them is that they are logically necessary. As
we have several times remarked, it is by insisting on
an impossible standard of perfection that the sceptic
makes himself secure.

This being so, we must be content with what we
have. In any particular case, if one's claim to know
what some other person is feeling be put in question,
one can uphold it by appealing to the evidence. What
we cannot do is to vindicate such claims in general,
any more than we can give a general vindication of our
trust in memory or in any form of record of the past.
Or rather, the general vindication comes out only in
the way in which the evidence is found to be sufficient
in particular instances. Further than this we cannot
go : it is enough if we can rebut the sceptic's arguments which are designed to show that we cannot even
go so far. Neither is this a purely negative achievement ; a matter of running hard in order to stay in
the same place. Our reward for taking scepticism

seriously is that we are brought to distinguish the different levels at which our claims to knowledge stand. In this way we gain a clearer understanding of the dimensions of our language ; and so of the world which it serves us to describe.

INDEX

255

THE END

PRINTED BY R. & R. CLARK, LTD., EDINBURGH